To-
Jack &
Robin

Luv Your All

Mom

MY DESCENT INTO DEATH

MY DESCENT INTO DEATH

A Second Chance at Life

HOWARD STORM

DOUBLEDAY

New York London Toronto Sydney Auckland

PUBLISHED BY DOUBLEDAY
a division of Random House, Inc.

DOUBLEDAY and the portrayal of an anchor with a dolphin are
registered trademarks of Random House, Inc.

Book design by Michael Collica

Library of Congress Cataloging-in-Publication Data
Storm, Howard.
My descent into death : a second chance at life / Howard Storm.—
1st U.S. ed.
p. cm.
Rev. ed. of: My descent into death and the message of love
that brought me back.
1. Storm, Howard. 2. Near-death experiences—Religious aspects—United
Church of Christ. 3. United Church of Christ—Clergy—Biography.
I. Storm, Howard. My descent into death and the message of love that
brought me back. II. Title.

BX9886.Z8S76 2005
133.9'01'3092—dc22
[B]
2004058257

ISBN 0-385-51376-3

March 2005
First U.S. Edition
First published in Great Britain by Clairview in 2000

3   5   7   9   10   8   6   4

CONTENTS

From the moment I glimpsed Howard Storm on television I knew he was extraordinary even among the "Near-Deathers," those unique individuals who, as the result of medical catastrophe, have been to the Other Side. Yes, he'd seen the Light they all talk about; yes, he'd experienced the personal life review so many mention; yes, he'd experienced the warmth and love of a higher being. But there was infinitely more to it for this man—as if that hadn't been enough. And he'd returned from death to alter the entire course of his life.

A career as an artist and teacher of art had been left behind for the Christian ministry, and it was obvious that Howard Storm's compulsion to talk about what had happened to him was ongoing. He was driven the way the saints of old were driven. He had been thrown down on the road to Damascus, and in each subsequent television appearance in which I saw him—and there were many—he appeared to be in the process of climbing to his feet from that Fall, struggling to testify to the momentous implications of what he'd seen. I wanted to find him, know him, beg him for more details. Only a deep inveterate respect for his privacy kept me from seeking him out.

When I finally discovered that he could and would write about his experiences, I was desperate for the material. And my expectations have been overwhelmingly surpassed. This book you have in hand is his most complete testimony to date. The story is beyond remarkable. Hell and Heaven are realized in these pages. The Lord Himself and His Angels are encountered. Storm sees the Universe beyond Time. Sure, others have told this story. That's the way it works. There are witnesses in all times and in many different places. Storm is a vital and enduring witness for here and for now. With a rare combination of sophistication and humility, Storm is able to lead us into a place of harrowing darkness and through his delivery from it by means of a simple if not primitive prayer. A realm of beatific light is revealed in all its splendor, and we are taken with Storm beyond time and doubt and care to the very secrets of the universe before the inevitable and painful return.

Make no mistake: this man's a mystic. This is a book that fulfills a calling. This is a book you devour from cover to cover, and pass on to others. This is a book you will quote in your daily conversation. Storm was meant to write it and we were meant to read it. Each Near-Death Experience changes the one who survives it. That one inevitably touches countless others. Storm's vocation is that he is meant to touch a great multitude; the loaves and fishes given to him will feed thousands if not hundreds of thousands. Such is his gift, and the gift to us.

—Anne Rice
New Orleans
January 2005

MY DESCENT INTO DEATH

1

PARIS

Paris, the City of Light. What could possibly go wrong in the heart of the civilized world? This was to be the next to last day of our art tour of Europe. Saturday morning began with a visit to Eugène Delacroix's home and studio. The studio contained Delacroix's palette, his easel, the chair he sat in, and his writing desk. Just my wife Beverly and I went to his studio because everyone else in the group wanted to sleep late, as they were getting pretty tired of being dragged around museums and galleries from morning till night. We arrived at the Delacroix Museum at nine, and just before eleven o'clock we returned to our hotel room to get our little group ready to go to the Georges Pompidou Center of Modern Art. This was to be one of the high points of the tour of Europe.

Back in the hotel room there was a feeling of nausea rising up inside me. A few times on our trip I had had indigestion and taken some over-the-counter antacid and aspirin tablets, which always alleviated the discomfort. Now I took two aspirin and washed them down with some stale Coke from the evening before and continued talking to one of the students, trying to ignore the growing discomfort in my stomach.

As I was talking to my student Monica about the day's plan, I felt as though I'd been shot. There was a searing pain in the middle of my stomach. My knees collapsed and I sank to the floor. I held my gut and screamed with pain. Something terrifying was happening inside me, and I didn't know what it was. I was surprised that there was no wound on the outside of my body. In fact, there had been no sound, and as I glanced about, there was no way a bullet could have entered the room. I looked up at the windows that opened onto the balcony. Morning sunlight was streaming through the closed glass of the balcony doors, filtered through the sheer curtains. There was no broken glass where I expected to see a bullet hole in the window, no ripped hole in the pristine curtain. There was only a wound deep inside my abdomen.

The pain was drowning me, like I was sinking into a lava pool of agony. As I thrashed about on the floor in desperate confusion, I searched feverishly for some explanation of what was happening to me. One minute I was talking with Monica about our upcoming museum visit and the next I was writhing on the floor, consumed with pain. I had collapsed at the foot of the bed but had wriggled my way into the narrow space between the wall and the bed. In terror, I struggled into a space where I would be safely wedged into a fetal position. Constricted between the bed and the wall, I struggled to control my rising panic. By screaming and groaning, I knew I was adding to my predicament and making it impossible for my wife to understand what was happening to me.

I screamed for my wife Beverly to get a doctor. She was numb with shock. I cursed at her when she didn't respond. She composed herself enough to call the hotel desk and was told that a doctor would be summoned immediately. From the floor I looked up at the full-length windows in the French doors to the balcony. Through the transparent white curtains, light was flooding into the little hotel room, and outside the sky was a brilliant cerulean blue. Somehow I felt reassured by the beauty of the day. Something was very wrong with me, but I took comfort in the fact that a doctor was on the way. This was Paris, the City of Light. I would be okay. As I waited, the pain kept getting worse. I tried to be stoic. I fought to control the gnawing terror.

In ten minutes the doctor arrived. He was slightly built and in his early thirties. I could resist only feebly as he struggled to pull me up onto the bed. He asked me what had happened as he opened the buttons of my shirt to examine my stomach. His probing fingers on my abdomen aggravated the pain. I fought against him. He said I had a perforation in my duodenum. I must go to a hospital right away.

"Will I need an operation?" I asked.

"Yes, immediately," he said. He phoned for an ambulance and then gave me a small amount of morphine by injection. The intense agony began to subside. He explained that the morphine was just enough to get me to the hospital, but wouldn't interfere with the anesthetic of the surgery that I would be having very soon.

It became possible to think more clearly. The hospital stay would be most inconvenient. Tomorrow my wife and I with the students on the tour were supposed to drive to Amsterdam for the return flight to America. But things would work out. I could manage. I always had.

The two young men who arrived with the ambulance appeared to be very pleasant. They lifted me from the bed and supported me on either side, carrying my weight on their shoulders.

We went down the hall and into a tiny hotel elevator that took us down to the first floor. There was barely enough room for us in the little elevator as I was propped up between them. The elevator stopped at the first floor, one floor above the street. From there, a long, winding staircase led down to street level. The ambulance attendants found a straight-back chair from the hotel dining room and carried me down the stairs. The men were straining to keep me aloft and balanced. I teetered and tottered as they struggled to carry me. I kept murmuring, "Please don't drop me." They laid me on a gurney at the sidewalk and then slid me into the back of a little ambulance. For a moment I panicked because I was afraid we were going to leave without my wife. To my great relief, I saw Beverly climb in the front seat beside the driver. The ambulance careened wildly through the Paris streets with its distinctive siren clearing a path through heavy midday traffic. I was reminded of scenes from World War II movies by the siren's sound, wailing mournfully through the congested streets of Paris.

After an amazing ride traveling at high speed, with the little ambulance swaying dangerously around each corner, we arrived at the emergency room of a large public hospital in Paris. I was immediately met by two young female doctors who began a thorough examination. One of the doctors looked like a young Jeanne Moreau. The other was thin and pale, with the saddest eyes. The intimacy of the examination they were doing was embarrassing. After consulting the X-ray films, they told me I had a large hole in my duodenum due to unknown causes, maybe an ulcer, maybe a foreign object. I must have an operation immediately or I would die. I asked if this could be done in America and was told I wouldn't survive the trip. They assured me that this was the best and biggest hospital in Paris. They were completely convincing as to the urgency of the situation and the necessity of the surgery.

They needed to get a tube into my stomach, but failed to tell me about the procedure. A big man straddled me and began to force a large aquarium-type tube down my nose. It slammed against the back of my throat, forcing a gag reaction. The more I gagged, the harder he shoved. Through the tears filling my eyes, I saw the thin doctor with the sad compassionate eyes make swallowing gestures with her hands, and I swallowed as hard as I could and the tube slid down.

I was still feeling the pain, but the morphine had taken the madness out of the terror. It was manageable now. As part of my effort to stay in control, I forced some weak laughter and made lame attempts at jokes. I was scared. I told my dear Beverly it would be okay. The doctors talked about a hospital stay of three or four weeks. Then there would be a couple of months of recovery at home.

Following the examination in the emergency department, I was taken by gurney out of the emergency building and rushed several blocks to the hospital building where the surgery would be performed. Every time the wheels banged against an imperfection in the concrete sidewalk, pain shot through my stomach, but I was comforted by the beauty of the surroundings. It was noon, the sun was shining, and it was the first day of June in the beautiful city of Paris, France. What could possibly go wrong?

We rode by elevator to a double room on the upper floor to await the operation. My roommate was a handsome elderly gentleman by the name of Monsieur Fleurin. He spoke English and was in his late sixties. His wife was visiting him. Her father had been an American who had come to France as a soldier during

World War I and stayed. Her English was excellent. She immediately tried to reassure me and comfort my frightened wife. Madame and Monsieur Fleurin were exceedingly handsome people and gracious to us frightened foreigners.

It was about noon and, after a flurry of activity, everything became calm. The bed I was given had no pillow, so Beverly made a roll of sheets to support my head. This was the beginning of the wait for the surgery, and the acute pain was gradually increasing. Jolts of stabbing, throbbing pain spread out into my torso. They took my breath away. The doctors told me to lie as still as possible, so as not to provoke the leaking hydrochloric acid and other juices that were digesting my insides.

At that time, what I did not know was that on weekends, Parisian hospitals are understaffed. Most doctors vacation on the coast of France or in the country. I later learned that there was only one surgeon on duty in the entire hospital complex! Only he could operate; only he could authorize any kind of medication. I never saw the surgeon that day, and since nurses in France have no authority to give medication, they were powerless to do anything for my increasingly grave condition.

In the emergency room they had inserted the large rubber tube through my nose and down into my stomach to suction out digestive fluids. It was very difficult to talk and my mouth became very dry; my mouth tasted like rubber. I wasn't allowed to drink anything to relieve the dryness. The pain in the center of my abdomen grew worse. The torment radiated out into my chest and down to the pelvis. Staying curled in a fetal position felt like the only way to keep the fire from radiating farther out into my extremities. Tears ran down my cheeks from the pain. The only sound I could make was an occasional low moan like an animal. Whenever I tried to talk, it agitated my abdomen and magnified the pain. It was best to lie perfectly still and focus on trying to breathe as quietly as possible.

Minutes stretched into hours. No doctor came. Whenever a nurse entered the room, I begged for morphine. There was nothing they could do. When they ignored my pleas, I asked Monsieur Fleurin to beg for me. I told the nurses that I was dying and I had Monsieur Fleurin do the same. In the middle of the afternoon, the nurse said she would contact a doctor to see what they could do and gave me an injection of a "stomach relaxant." It had no effect whatsoever. Every time Beverly or I asked the nurses about the operation, they said it would be done within the hour. By early afternoon the relief from the morphine I had been given at the hotel had worn off completely. The fiery pain grew steadily worse. My stomach felt like it was full of burning coals. Hot flashes of intense pain shot into my arms and legs. I kept repeating in French that I was dying and begged for morphine over and over again.

I kept thinking that I should be unconscious because of my condition. Nothing in my life had prepared me for this intense agony. Why didn't I black out? What had I ever done to deserve this?

The nurse became increasingly impatient with our questions and pleas. Beverly was told that if she didn't stop her demands, she would be put out of the room. My poor beautiful wife could do nothing for me, and she couldn't get anyone to lift a finger to help me. She was acutely aware that she was losing me, and there was nothing she could do about it in spite of all her pleas.

In hindsight I realize that this woeful lack of attention resulted not from malice, but rather from bureaucratic ineptitude and indifference. I also realize that because I did not express the agony I was experiencing more dramatically, the staff didn't realize the full extent of my crisis.

My whole life had been one of self-sufficient stoicism. I believed I didn't need anyone's help. I could handle anything. I could do this, I thought.

In my extreme pain, seconds seemed like minutes and minutes seemed like hours. Minute by minute, second by second, the time passed into hours. By eight o'clock that evening the pain had become totally unbearable. I'd been in the same bed, in the same position, in the same room since noon without ever seeing a doctor. The pain didn't come and go in waves anymore, it just got worse and worse. The hydrochloric acid leaking from my stomach was spreading throughout my abdominal cavity and literally eating me up from the inside. The searing torment was gaining strength and I was getting weaker. Breathing was almost impossible. I tried to pour every bit of energy into inhaling and exhaling to stay alive. It was vividly clear to me that if I failed to breathe, it would be the end of my life. Period. I was so weakened from the ordeal, I knew there was very little strength left in me.

I kept thinking, this is not how it's supposed to end. I was fading away in a Paris hospital and they were indifferent to my agony. Why didn't they care? What would happen to my wife, my two children, my paintings, my house, my gardens—all the things I cared about? I was thirty-eight years old and just beginning to achieve some fame as an artist. Had all my work and struggle come to this?

I had grown so frail that I could hardly lift my head or speak. Beverly looked drained, totally emotionally exhausted. I didn't want to tell her that I knew the end was near. I told her I couldn't hold on much longer. It had gotten very dark outside the window of the bare hospital room.

I was later told by American doctors back in the United States that from the time of the perforation, my life expectancy was about five hours. The condition I had was similar to a burst appendix. Sometime around nine o'clock, one of the nurses came into the room. She said the doctor had gone home and the operation couldn't be performed until the next morning. I knew I wouldn't survive until then. Ten hours had now passed since the hole in my stomach erupted. I had fought as long and as hard as I could to stay alive. I had nothing left. It was impossible to muster the strength to breathe anymore.

I knew I was dying now. I knew that dying was the only way out of this world of pain. To die was the easiest thing in the world. All I would have to do was stop fighting to breathe in, breathe out. I turned to Beverly, who had been crying for hours, and I had never seen her look so distressed. Fighting against the flood of tears, I told her that I loved her very much. I told her it was over. We said our good-byes to each other. I didn't have the courage or strength to say more. She got up from her chair next to the bed and put her arms around me. She kissed me and told me that she loved me and she would always love me, and then she said good-bye. She sat back down and cried from the core of her being.

Saying to myself, "Let it end now," I closed my eyes. The last thing I saw was Beverly's throbbing shoulders and her hands pressed over her eyes as I went into oblivion. I knew that what would happen next would be the end of any kind of conscious-ness or existence. I knew that to be true. The idea of any kind of life after death never entered my mind because I didn't believe in that kind of thing. I knew for certain that there was no such thing as life after death. Only simpleminded people believed in that sort of thing. I didn't believe in God, or heaven, or hell, or any other fairy tales. I drifted into darkness, a sleep into annihilation.

2

THE DESCENT

I was standing up. I opened my eyes to see why I was standing up. I was between the two hospital beds in the hospital room. This wasn't right. Why was I alive? I had wanted oblivion, escape from the all-consuming, unbearable pain.

"Could this be a dream?" I kept thinking. "This has got to be a dream." But I knew that it wasn't. I was aware that I felt more alert, more aware, and more alive than I had ever felt in my entire life. All my senses were extremely vivid. Everything around and in me was alive. The linoleum tiles on the floor were slick and cool and my bare feet felt moist and clammy against them. The bright light of the room illuminated every detail in crystal clarity. The mix of odors of stale urine, sweat, residue of bleach from the sheets, and enamel paint filled my nostrils. The sounds of my breathing and the blood rushing through my veins hummed in my ears. The surface of my skin tingled with the sensations of air moving across it. My mouth tasted stale and dry. How bizarre to feel all of my senses heightened and alert, as if I had just been born. Thoughts raced through my mind. "This is no dream. I am more alive than I have ever been."

This is too real. I squeezed my fists and was amazed how much I was feeling in my hands just by making a fist. I could feel the bones in my hands, the muscles expand and contract, skin pressed against skin. I touched my body with my hands in several places and everything was intact, alive. My head, shoulders, arms, abdomen, and thighs were all intact. I pinched myself and it hurt. I was aware of the problem in my stomach, but it was not as severe as before. It was more of a memory of the pain. I was profoundly aware of my situation and of the necessity of having an operation as soon as possible. In every respect, I was more alive than I had ever been in my life.

I looked at my roommate, Monsieur Fleurin, and his eyes were half closed. I turned and looked at Beverly sitting in the chair next to my bed. She was motionless, staring at the floor. She looked physically exhausted and emotionally drained. I spoke to her but she didn't seem to hear. She sat absolutely motionless. I gave up trying to talk to her for the moment because something between us caught my attention.

There was an object in the bed under the sheet. As I bent over to look at the face of the body in the bed, I was horrified to see the resemblance that it had to my own face. It was impossible that that thing could be me because I was standing over it and looking at it. I was looking down at a facsimile of my hands, arms, torso, legs, and feet under the sheet. It looked like my face, but it looked so meaningless, like a husk, empty and lifeless. I was standing there next to the bed and staring at the object in the bed. Everything that was me, my consciousness and physical being, was standing next to the bed. No, it wasn't me lying in the bed, it was just a thing that didn't have any importance to me. It may as well have been a slab of meat in the supermarket.

The impossibility of the situation set my mind reeling. It occurred to me that I must have gone crazy. Somehow I had split my being into two parts. I was schizophrenic, completely mad, delusional. Yet I had never felt more alert and conscious. I wanted desperately to get through to Beverly, and I started yelling for her to say something, but she remained frozen in the chair next to the bed. I screamed and raged at her, but she just ignored me. No matter how loudly I yelled or cursed at her, there was no reaction. Her eyes didn't even blink. It was impossible that she couldn't hear me screaming.

I turned around to Monsieur Fleurin in the bed behind me. I bent over him and yelled inches from his face, "Why are you ignoring me?" He looked right through me as though I were not even there. I could see the droplets of spittle hitting his face as I screamed at him. He stared right through me as if I were invisible. Nothing worked the way it was supposed to. I became increasingly upset as anger, fear, and confusion filled me.

The hospital room was brightly lit. Everything was vividly clear. All of the details of the room were extremely sharp and distinct. Every nuance in the linoleum floor, every bump in the paint on the steel bed was magnified. I had never viewed the world with such clarity and exactness. Everything was in such extreme focus that it was overwhelming. My sense of taste and touch and temperature were exploding. The taste in my mouth was revolting because it was so overpowering. "What's happening to me? This is so real! But how can this be?"

Maybe, I thought, they had built a wax replica of me while I was unconscious. They could have made a quick-drying mold of my face and put it on a dummy while I was out and put it in the bed. But why would they do that? Is this some kind of test to see how I would react? This doesn't make any sense. How else could this happen?

Off in the distance, outside the room in the hall, I heard voices calling me. "Howard, Howard," they were calling. They were pleasant voices, male and female, young and old, calling me in English. None of the hospital staff spoke English so clearly; they couldn't pronounce the name "Howard" very well. I was hopelessly confused. Beverly and Monsieur Fleurin didn't seem to hear them. I asked who they were and what they wanted.

"Come out here," they said. "Let's go, hurry up. We've been waiting for you for a long time."

"I can't," I said. "I'm sick. Something's the matter with me; something's wrong in here. I need an operation. I am very sick!"

"We can get you fixed up," they said. "If you hurry up. Don't you want to get better? Don't you want help?"

I was in an unknown hospital in a foreign country, in an extremely bizarre situation, and I was afraid of those people calling me. They were irritated by my questions, which were only attempts to find out who they were. The hallway looked strange as I moved closer to the door. I had a feeling that if I left the room, it might be impossible to get back in. But I couldn't communicate with my wife and I couldn't communicate with my roommate. The voices continued to say, "We can't help you if you don't come out here." After more unanswered questions, I assumed they must be here to take me to my operation. Who else could they be? I decided to follow them rather than remain in a room where everyone ignored me. After all, I needed surgery.

I stepped out into the hall, full of anxiety. The area seemed to be light but very hazy, like a television screen with terrible reception. I couldn't make out any details. It was like being in a plane passing through thick clouds. The people were off in the distance and I couldn't see them very clearly. But I could tell that they were male and female, tall and short, old and young adults.

Their clothes were gray and they were pale. As I tried to get close to them to identify them, they quickly withdrew deeper into the fog. So I had to follow farther and farther into the thick atmosphere. I could never get closer to them than ten feet. I had lots of questions. Who were they? What did they want? Where did they want me to go? What was the matter with my wife? How could this be real? They wouldn't answer anything. Their only response was to insist that I hurry up and follow them.

They told me repeatedly that my problems were meaningless and unnecessary. In emotional distress, I followed them, shuffling along in my bare feet with the memory of the pain in my belly, feeling very much alive. I was moist with perspiration, quite confused, but not at all tired. I knew that I had a problem that must be operated on right away. They appeared to be my only hope.

Every time I hesitated, they demanded that I keep up. They continued to repeat the promise that if I followed them, my troubles would end. We walked on and on, and my repeated inquiries were rebuffed. They insisted on hurrying to get to our destination.

During the journey, I attempted to count how many of these people there were and figure out something about their individual identities, but I couldn't. The fog thickened as we went on, and it became gradually darker. They moved around me and their numbers seemed to be increasing. I was confused about the direction we were taking. I knew that we had been traveling for miles, but I had the strange ability to occasionally look back and see through the doorway of the hospital room, although the door was getting smaller and smaller. That body was still there, lying motionless on the bed. Beverly was sitting there as frozen as she had been when this surreal experience first began. It seemed many miles away, but I could still see it off in the distance.

All the while we were walking, I was trying to pick up some clues as to where we were going by what we were walking on. There were no walls of any kind. The floor or ground had no features; there was no incline or decline. It was like walking on a smooth, slightly damp, cool floor. How could this hospital hallway be so long? How could this same unvarying plane go on forever? When would we go uphill or downhill? Sometimes I had a strange feeling that we might be subtly descending.

I also couldn't make out how much time was passing. There was a profound sense of timelessness. This was strange because, as a teacher, I had been able to estimate when I had talked for a certain length of time. I only knew that it seemed like we had been walking a long, long while. I kept asking when we were going to get there. "I'm sick," I said. "I can't do this." They became increasingly angry and sarcastic. "If you'd quit moaning and groaning, we'd get there," they said. "Move it, let's go, hurry up!" The more questioning and suspicious I became, the more antagonistic and authoritarian they became. They were whispering about my bare rear end, which wasn't covered by my hospital gown, and about how pathetic I was. I knew they were talking about me, but when I tried to hear exactly what they were saying, they would say to one another, "Shhh, he can hear you, he can hear you."

They didn't appear to know what I was thinking, and I didn't know what they were thinking. What was increasingly clear to me was that they were deceiving me. The longer I stayed with them, the further away escape would be.

Back in the hospital room, an eternity before, I had hoped to die and end the torment of life. Now I was being forced by a mob of unfeeling people toward some unknown destination in the encroaching darkness. They began shouting and hurling insults at me, demanding that I hurry along. The more miserable I became, the more enjoyment they derived from my distress.

A terrible sense of dread was growing within me. This experience was *too* real. In some ways I was more aware and sensitive than I had ever been. Everything that was happening couldn't be possible, yet it was happening. This was not a dream or hallucination, but I wished that it were. Everything I had experienced before this was a dream compared to the way that I was now experiencing reality. I was frightened, exhausted, cold, and lost. It was clear that the help these terrible beings had first promised was just a ruse to trick me into following them. I was reluctant to go farther, but any hesitation on my part brought abuse and insults. They told me we were almost there, to shut up and take a few more steps.

A few of the voices attempted a conciliatory tone that amused the others. Among themselves the mood was one of excitement and triumph.

For a long time I had been walking with my gaze down to watch my step. When I looked around I was horrified to discover that we were in complete darkness.

The hopelessness of my situation overwhelmed me. I told them I would go no farther, to leave me alone, and that they were liars. I could feel their breath on me as they shouted and snarled insults. Then they began to push and shove me about. I began to fight back. A wild frenzy of taunting, screaming, and hitting ensued. I fought like a wild man. As I swung and kicked at them, they bit and tore back at me. All the while it was obvious that they were having great fun. Even though I couldn't see anything in the darkness, I was aware that there were dozens or hundreds of them all around and over me. My attempts to fight back only provoked greater merriment. As I continued to defend myself, I was aware that they weren't in any hurry to annihilate me. They were playing with me just as a cat plays with a mouse. Every new assault brought howls of cacophonous laughter. They began to tear off pieces of my flesh. To my horror, I realized that I was being taken apart and eaten alive, methodically, slowly, so that their entertainment would last as long as possible.

While I couldn't see in this total darkness, every sound and every physical sensation registered with horrifying intensity.

These creatures were once human beings. The best way I can describe them is to think of the worst imaginable person stripped of every impulse of compassion. Some of them seemed to be able to tell others what to do, but I had no sense of there being any organization to the mayhem. They didn't appear to be controlled or directed by anyone. Simply, they were a mob of beings totally driven by unbridled cruelty.

In that darkness I had intense physical contact with them when they swarmed over me. Their bodies felt exactly as human bodies do except for two characteristics. They had very long, sharp fingernails, and their teeth were longer than normal. I'd never been bitten by a human being before this.

During our struggle they felt no pain. Other than their lack of feeling, they appeared to possess no special abilities. During my initial experience with them they were clothed. In our intimate physical contact I never felt any clothing.

The level of noise was excruciating. Countless people laughed, yelled, and jeered. In the middle of this bedlam I was the object of their desire. My torment was their excitement. The more I fought, the greater their thrill.

Eventually I became too badly torn up and too broken to resist. Most of them gave up tormenting me because I was no longer amusing, but a few still picked and gnawed at me and ridiculed me for no longer being amusing. I had been torn apart. In that wretched state I lay there in the darkness.

I haven't described everything that happened. There are things that I don't care to remember. In fact, much that occurred was simply too gruesome and disturbing to recall. I've spent years trying to suppress a lot of it. After the experience, whenever I did remember those details, I would become traumatized.

3

ALONE

As I lay on the ground, my tormentors swarming around me, a voice emerged from my chest. It sounded like my voice, but it wasn't a thought of mine. I didn't say it. The voice that sounded like my voice, but wasn't, said, "Pray to God." I remember thinking, "Why? What a stupid idea. That doesn't work. What a cop-out. Lying here in this darkness, surrounded by hideous creatures, I don't believe in God. This is utterly hopeless, and I am beyond any possible help whether I believe in God or not. I don't pray, period."

A second time, the voice spoke to me, "Pray to God." It was recognizably my voice, but I had not spoken. Pray how? Pray what? I hadn't prayed at any time in my entire adult life. I didn't know how to pray. I wouldn't know what the right words were even if I could pray. I can't pray!

That voice said it again, "Pray to God!" It was more definite this time. I wasn't sure what to do. Praying, for me as a child, had been something I had watched adults doing. It was something fancy and had to be done just so. I tried to remember prayers from my childhood experiences in Sunday school. Prayer was something you memorized. What could I remember from so long ago? Tentatively, I murmured a few lines—a jumble from the Twenty-third Psalm, "The Star-Spangled Banner," the Lord's Prayer, the Pledge of Allegiance, and "God Bless America," and whatever other churchly sounding phrases came to mind.

"Yea, though I walk in the valley of the shadow of death, I will fear no evil, for thou art with me. For purple mountain majesty, mine eyes have seen the glory of the coming of the Lord. Deliver us from evil. One nation under God. God Bless America."

To my amazement, the cruel, merciless beings tearing the life out of me were incited to rage by my ragged prayer. It was as if I were throwing boiling oil on them. They screamed at me, "There is no God! Who do you think you're talking to? Nobody can hear you! Now we are really going to hurt you." They spoke in the most obscene language, worse than any blasphemy said on earth. But at the same time, they were backing away. I could still hear their voices in the utter darkness, but they were getting more and more distant. I realized that saying things about God was actually driving them away. I became a little more forceful with what I was saying. "Yea, though I walk through the valley of death, God is going to get you. Leave me alone, the Lord is my shepherd, and one nation under God, and . . ." Retreating, they became more rabid, cursing and screaming against God. They claimed that what I was praying was worthless and that I was a coward, a nothing. In time they retreated back into the distant gloom, beyond my hearing. I knew they were far away but could return.

I was alone, destroyed, and yet painfully alive in this revoltingly horrible place. I had no idea where I was. At first, when I was walking with these people, I had thought we were in some foggy part of the hospital. In time, I realized we had gone somewhere else. Now I didn't know if I was even in the world. How could *this* be the world?

There was no indication of a direction to follow even if I had been physically able to crawl. The agony that I had suffered during the day in the hospital was nothing compared to what I was feeling now. The all-consuming physical pain was secondary to the emotional pain. Their psychological cruelty to me was unbearable.

I was alone in that darkness for time without measure. I thought about what I had done. All my life I had thought that hard work was what counted. My life was devoted to building a monument to my ego. My family, my sculptures, my painting, my house, my gardens, my little fame, my illusions of power, were all an extension of my ego. All of those things were gone now, and what did they matter? All those things that I had lived for were lost to me, and they didn't mean a thing.

All of my adult life I had been strong and confident that I could take care of myself. Now I was a worm cast into the outer darkness and had neither any strength nor power, nor my inner rage, to protect me. This ordeal had stripped me of all of my defenses.

All of my life, I'd fought a constant undertone of anxiety, fear, dread, and angst. If I could become famous, I could defeat powerlessness and beat death. But if I didn't become famous, then I'd die and my whole life would be meaningless. So I didn't live in the present. I had always striven for an unattainable eternal fame as my protection against oblivion. The pit of despair I was now in gave me neither fame nor oblivion. I was stuck with myself, and it was frightening.

I hadn't had time for many friends. I was too busy. As a matter of fact, I found most people to be a tiresome nuisance. I did what I could to avoid social interactions. I didn't belong to any clubs or organizations. In spite of the narcissistic appearance, I didn't like myself, and I didn't like other people, either.

How ironic it was to end up in the sewer of the universe with people who fed off the pain of others! I had had little genuine compassion for others. It dawned on me that I was not unlike these miserable creatures that had tormented me. Failing truly to love, they had been led into the outer darkness where their only desire was to inflict their inner torment onto another. Devoid of love, hope, and faith, they craved intimacy but found it only to be more torment. Any mention of God, whom they had rejected, enraged them. These debased people may have been successful in the world, but they had missed the most important thing of all, and now were reaping what they had sown.

I believed that if you were born into this dog-eat-dog kind of world, you might as well be a winner instead of a loser. All the people I knew were out for themselves. Rather than get the dregs, I'd go for the good things. So what if I was ambitious? Anyone who wasn't pragmatic and realistic about life (like me) was a fool.

Being an artist was a way to get what I wanted. You win eternal fame as an artist. They display your work in marble temples and worship it for thousands of years. I wanted to be famous for hundreds and thousands of years. People would read books about me and say, "Howard Storm, the great artist."

I viewed people who were religious with contempt. I thought they believed in fairy tales because they couldn't cope with the harsh reality of life. They had bought into a fantasy in order to justify their mediocrity. If that's what it takes to make them feel good, let them wallow in it. I was in the mainstream of my culture. I had no faith, no hope, and no reliance on anyone, just survival of the fittest. My colleagues at the university (the ones I associated with) thought about life the way I did. I was in good company. Man was the measure of all things. We knew what was real and what wasn't. If any students or colleagues had other ideas, they didn't talk to me about them. They recognized a dyed-in-the-wool cynic when they met one.

I was in control of my life. I believed in being a law-abiding person and that you should avoid going to jail at all costs. I didn't rob banks or murder anyone. I lived within the law of the land and obeyed the unwritten rules of civility. Wasn't this sufficient for a good life? The rugged individualism that I had learned from my father, my schooling, and my American culture was my religion. Why would I need to believe in a higher power? Who would put the needs of others ahead of their own needs? You have to watch your back always. Life is every man for himself. The one who dies with the most toys wins. Compassion is for the weak. If you don't take care of yourself, nobody else will. I thought I was the biggest, baddest bear in the woods. Wasn't I good enough?

I didn't believe in a life after death. When you died, it was like having the switch turned off. That was it, the end of your existence, finished, just darkness.

Now I was in that darkness, beyond life, and it was hell.

I knew then that this was the absolute end of my existence in the world, and it was more horrible than anything I could possibly have imagined. It would have been much better to die in the hospital than live in this despicable garbage heap. I felt like a match whose flame had been spent and the ember was slowly dying away to nothing. Little strength was left to resist becoming a creature gnashing his teeth in the outer darkness. I wasn't far from becoming like one of my own tormentors for all eternity.

4

THE LIGHT

L ying there, torn apart, inside and out, I knew I was lost. I would never see the world again. I was left alone to become a creature of the dark.

Then for the first time in my adult life a very old tune from childhood started going through my head. It was my voice, but it sounded like a little boy singing the same line over and over again. The child that I had once been was singing full of innocence, trust, and hope. "Jesus loves me, da da da . . ." There was only that bit of the tune and those few words that I could remember. We had sung those words in Sunday school when I was a child.

Somewhere out there in that vast darkness there could be something good. There is someone who might love me. I didn't have any theological interest about what it meant. It was simply a spontaneous recollection from my Sunday school days: Jesus loves me. Jesus loves me. Jesus loves me.

I desperately needed someone to love me, someone to know I was alive. A ray of hope began to dawn in me, a belief that there really was something greater out there. For the first time in my adult life I wanted it to be true that Jesus loved me. I didn't know how to express what I wanted and needed, but with every bit of my last ounce of strength, I yelled out into the darkness, "Jesus, save me." I yelled that from the core of my being with all the energy I had left. I have never meant anything more strongly in my life.

Far off in the darkness I saw a pinpoint of light like the faintest star in the sky. I wondered why I hadn't seen it before. The star was rapidly getting brighter and brighter. At first I thought it might be some *thing,* not someone. It was moving toward me at an alarming rate. As it came closer, I realized that I was right in its path and I might be consumed by its brilliance. I couldn't take my eyes off it; the light was more intense and more beautiful than anything I had ever seen. It was brighter than the sun, brighter than a flash of lightning. Soon the light was upon me. I knew that while it was indescribably brilliant, it wasn't just light. This was a living being, a luminous being approximately eight feet tall and surrounded by an oval of radiance. The brilliant intensity of the light penetrated my body. Ecstasy swept away the agony. Tangible hands and arms gently embraced me and lifted me up. I slowly rose up into the presence of the light and the torn pieces of my body miraculously healed before my eyes. All my wounds vanished and I became whole and well in the light. More important, the despair and pain were replaced by love. I had been lost and now was found; I had been dead and now was alive.

This loving, luminous being who embraced me knew me intimately. He knew me better than I knew myself. He was knowledge and wisdom. I knew that he knew everything about me. I was unconditionally loved and accepted. He was King of Kings, Lord of Lords, Christ Jesus the Savior. Jesus does love me, I thought.

I experienced love in such intensity that nothing I had ever known before was comparable. His love was greater than all human love put together. His love totally enveloped me, and I realized that he was indescribably wonderful: goodness, power, knowledge, and love. He was more loving than one can begin to imagine or describe. Jesus *did* indeed love me.

This person of blinding glory loved me with overwhelming power. After what I had been through, to be completely known, accepted, and intensely loved by this beautiful God/man of light surpassed anything I had ever known or could possibly have imagined. I had called out to Jesus and he came to rescue me. I cried and cried from joy, and the tears kept coming. Joy upon joy billowed through me. He held me and caressed me like a mother with her baby, like a father with his long-lost prodigal son. I cried all the tears of a lifetime of hopelessness and tears of shame over my unbelief. I cried all the tears of joy and salvation. I cried like a baby and couldn't stop crying.

He held me close and stroked my back. We rose upward, gradually at first, and then like a rocket we shot out of that dark and detestable hell. We traversed an enormous distance, light-years, although very little time elapsed. I tried to regain my composure because it was embarrassing to be crying so hard. Tears had soaked my face and mucus poured from my nose. I tried to stop my blubbering, and I turned and looked toward the direction we were moving.

Off in the distance far, far away, I saw a vast area of illumination that looked like a galaxy. In the center was an enormously bright concentration of light. Outside the center, countless millions of spheres of light were flying about, entering and leaving that great concentration of light at the center. This was comparable to seeing the sky at night on the top of a mountain with the stars so abundant that they almost touch one another. These "stars" were all in motion in relation to the center. They were moving toward or away from the brilliant white center of the universe.

As we approached, still a vast distance away, I was permeated with tangible intense feelings and thoughts of love. While moving toward the presence of the great light, center of all being, The One, I was beyond thought. It is not possible to articulate what occurred. Simply, I knew that God loved me, that God loved creation, that God is love. This experience of love totally changed my life from the inside out. No matter what happened, I would always know that God loved me.

I began to be aware of my separate self, and I became very ashamed and afraid. How many times in my life had I denied and scoffed at the reality before me? How many thousands of times had I used the name of God as a curse? What incredible arrogance to use the name of God as an insult. Such a travesty against all that is holy. I was terribly ashamed to go closer. The wonderful, incredible intensity of the emanations of goodness and love might be more than I could bear.

I felt like garbage, filthy rags, in the presence of the Holy One. My friend carrying me, Jesus, my best friend, was aware of my fear and reluctance and shame. I thought to myself, "I am scum that belongs back down in the sewer. They have made a terrible mistake. I don't belong here."

For the first time, he spoke. He spoke directly to my mind in his young male voice. "We don't make mistakes, and you do belong here." So we stopped where we were, still countless light-years away from the great supreme being in heaven. I cried from shame, and he comforted me.

Then Jesus called out in a musical tone to some of the luminous entities radiating from the great center. Several came and circled around us. The radiance emanating from them contained exquisite colors of a range and intensity far exceeding anything I had seen before. It was like looking at the iridescence in the deep brilliance of a diamond. We simply do not have the words to express their beauty. When you look into a bright light, the intensity hurts your eyes. These beings were far brighter than the most powerful searchlight, yet I could look at them with no sense of discomfort. In fact, their radiance penetrated me; I could feel it inside me and through me, and it made me feel wonderful. It was ecstasy. These were the saints and angels.

They knew everything I was thinking. I didn't know whether I would be capable of controlling my thoughts. I could hear their individual voices in my mind as they addressed me. I thought, "What if I say something I don't want you to hear?" And no sooner had I thought that than I thought the word "breast." They all laughed and told me that they knew everything I had ever thought and that I couldn't surprise them. I was both embarrassed and relieved.

I heard their voices clearly and individually. Each had a distinct personality, but they spoke directly to my mind, not through my ears. And they used normal colloquial English. Everything that I thought, they knew immediately. It was in this way that we conversed.

"You're upset. What can we do to help you?"

"I don't belong here."

"You do belong here."

"You've got the wrong person. I don't belong here."

"This is right. It's all been for this moment. We can appear to you in our human form if you wish or in any form you want, so you will be comfortable with us."

The last thing I wanted to see was people because I had had enough of people after what had happened to me. I hated people. For them to become human in appearance meant that they would have to turn down their radiance. This would be an insult to their glorious appearance.

"No. Please don't change into anything for me. You're more beautiful than anything I've ever seen."

They all seemed to know and understand me and to be completely familiar with my thoughts and my past. No one could know me more intimately. It was like going to a large gathering of relatives at Christmas and not being quite able to remember their names or to whom they are married or how they are related; but you do know that you are with family. I don't know if they were my relatives or not. It felt like they were closer to me than anyone I had ever known.

I was ashamed when I realized that I was naked, and I covered myself with my hands. They were amused and told me that they had seen me many times and that I had nothing to hide from them. I tried to relax.

_____

5

LIFE REVIEW

When I was in the company of Jesus and the angels, they asked me if I would like to see my life. Unsure of what to expect, I agreed. The record of my life was their record, not my memory of my life. We watched and experienced episodes that were from the point of view of a third party. The scenes they showed me were often of incidents I had forgotten. They showed their effects on people's lives, of which I'd had no previous knowledge. They reported the thoughts and feelings of people I had interacted with, which I had been unaware of at the time. They showed me scenes from my life that I would not have chosen, and they eliminated scenes from my life that I wanted them to see. It was a complete surprise to see how my life history was being presented.

Seven angels and myself held by Jesus were arranged in a circle while the scenes were projected in the midst of the circle. The images were primarily of people and a few inanimate objects that located the event's time and place. It was similar to a play without scenery except for the bare essentials. The drama was in chronological order and very selective, demonstrating to me the important developments in my spiritual growth in the world.

We began with scenes of my birth and infancy. The powerful feelings of love that my parents had for me were overwhelming. My parents had unbounded good intentions for their third child, who was their first and only son. My father had returned from service in the navy during World War II and had bought a new, small house in a suburban development. He was thirty-six and my mother was twenty-six. They both looked younger than I remembered them. They were happily living the American dream with two daughters and a son in a little Cape house in suburban Boston. The scenes of my infancy and early childhood were idyllic and filled with love.

We saw scenes of tension develop. As our family grew, my father's career as a salesman for an international flour milling company put increasing demands on his time. My mother, a nurse, began to work nights to increase the family income so that we could escalate our social status. The neighborhood we lived in was composed of similar families seeking upward mobility. Our extended family was an important part of our weekly obligations.

My father had been a lieutenant in the navy and wanted a highly disciplined home life. My mother had been raised in a very strict Lutheran Finnish immigrant home and accepted her husband's complete authority over the running of the family. The house was immaculate, and dinner was elaborate and formal. My sisters and I were taught to be well mannered and docile. My father gave commands and the family obeyed promptly.

I saw how I was being trained to repress emotions and was obedient so as to win the approval of my parents. I was also learning that my father completely dominated all of us by the threat of his anger. Although we were not allowed to show anger, I was learning what a powerful means of controlling people anger could be.

In every scene of my childhood, I could feel my intense desire for approval and love. It appeared from the scenes of my childhood that I was driven by a need to be loved while I explored and discovered the world around me. I would work hard in school to win approval from teachers. Teachers who made me feel loved got everything I had to give in return. Teachers who didn't love me only frustrated me in my need to be perfect for them.

The angels showed me how my father's compulsion to be successful was driving him toward increasing impatience and rage with his family. I saw how my mother, sisters, and I each developed different means of coping with his unpredictable mood swings. My mother was increasingly passive but withdrawing emotionally from him. My sisters were developing elaborate characters of hypocrisy and duplicity. I grew withdrawn and lived in a private world full of anger and violence.

The angels were showing me how important love was in shaping each member of the family's character. They shared their sadness as we saw how love was expressed in inappropriate ways.

The angels, Jesus, and I felt such disappointment as we watched a typical scene of my father coming home from work late in the evening full of anger. My sisters and I tried to avoid him as much as possible so we wouldn't get yelled at for some capital offense like slouching or putting an elbow on the table. Getting slapped in the face without warning or provocation was becoming common. How pitiful it was to watch a child, who just wanted to be loved, get physical and emotional abuse for no reason. As these scenes of family dysfunction increased over the years, I saw love turn to hate in people who really wanted to be loved.

Watching these scenes of our deteriorating family, I wanted to intervene, but it was only a record of what had happened and couldn't be altered in any way. The angels and Jesus shared their feelings of joy with me when love was expressed, and they shared their disappointment and sadness when we hurt one another. God had put my mother, father, sisters, and me together to love and support one another in our life's journey to grow in love and spirit. We were adapting our desire to love in unhealthy ways.

We watched scenes of my life as I became an adolescent. I became increasingly rebellious, and it was painful to see how I hurt my father by emotionally rejecting him. The more we fought, the more our relationship deteriorated. It was a surprise to see how I had contributed to this hostility and was not the innocent victim I had imagined myself to be. I sought love and support from adult male figures who were kind. I excelled in the shot put and discus for a track coach who gave me acceptance and approval. The angels and Jesus had no interest in the track meet competitions I won or lost. They were interested in the relationships and how we encouraged or hurt one another.

The advent of rock and roll music carried a message that my adolescent mind was eager to accept: love is romantic sexual relations with members of the opposite sex. I readily began the pursuit of girlfriends. It was possible to fall in love with a succession of like-minded girls. The music, television, movies, magazines, and books were bombarding us with this message of love.

The problem with the cultural climate was that it identified love exclusively with sexual relations. I didn't understand—nor did my generation—that love and sexual relations are not the same thing. We viewed members of the opposite sex as objects to be exploited for sexual gratification. Relations between male friends were always aggressive because we were rivals for the females. Spiritually, this was a disaster for me and for my generation. We had fun but we were unhappy because we were looking for love in all the wrong places.

Church, school, and home became irrelevant to life's pursuit of love because they refused to discuss sexuality and the other topics relevant to our adolescent lives. This period of my life was shameful to watch in divine company because I had misdirected my desire to love and be loved. God is not particularly interested in human sexual expression. God is interested in how we love one another and doesn't want us to exploit one another. The sexual revolution that I grew up in was opposed to love by promoting counterfeit sexual love as true love. This cultural wave of hedonism was bathed in alcohol and drugs, which are an even further departure from love and the will of God.

It was amazing to see that God had chosen a woman to love me and for me to love her. In time, we married and have had the most intimate, difficult, wonderful opportunity to learn the true meaning of love with each other. God brought my wife and me together to learn love. I saw it in my life review. God gives us each other to learn how to love. This is our job. It became painfully clear that I was to be God's instrument to love this woman and she is God's instrument to love me. How often we saw examples of when I had been loving, and too often we watched examples of when I had been controlling. Dominance is not love. Love supports.

They showed me how God had given us the opportunity to

learn love by having children and raising them to be loving. In my life review, I had to turn away numerous times when I saw myself treating my children in unloving ways. The most unloving thing that I did was to be at times so obsessed with my concerns that I was indifferent to their needs. I am sorry for the occasions that I was impatient or cruel to my daughter and son. The most disturbing behaviors I witnessed in my life review were the times when I cared more about my career as an artist and college professor than about their need to be loved. The emotional abandonment of my children was devastating to review.

It was horrifying to see how I had become so much like my father, putting status and success above everything else. I believed that my worth was measured by my success in my chosen career. Because others determine one's degree of success, one learns to value oneself based on the criteria of others. Of course, one is never good enough because there is always a critic and another level of achievement to conquer. This becomes a never-ending quest for the unattainable goal of approval. The more you succeed, the more driven you are to prove your worth. I bought into this game hook, line, and sinker. I was caught dangling on the strings others pulled, missing the simple love and joy of wife and family.

When the angels showed me how destructive this was to the well-being of my loved ones, I wanted to end my life review. They insisted that I needed to see the truth of my life and learn from it. I begged them to stop it because I was so ashamed of my failure to live lovingly and because of the grief I had caused God, Jesus, and the heavenly beings. The only reason I could bear to proceed with the life review was because of their love for me. No matter what we watched me do in life, they communicated their love for me, even as they expressed their disapproval of things I did.

One of the things I had done repeatedly in my life was blaspheme God. During my home life and later as an art student, I had acquired the habit of swearing profusely. This became an unconscious habit and meant nothing to me. To use vulgar words is only poor taste. To use the name of God in crude or empty ways is an insult to our Creator. I was horrified at how it hurt my heavenly company when we witnessed me blaspheming God and Christ Jesus in my life review.

My life review had begun in my infancy, and it was a joy to see my mother and father young and happy, loving their child. As the life review progressed from adolescence into adulthood, there were moments of joy when I saw that I had been compassionate and moments of displeasure when I saw that I had been selfish and cruel. As my adult life unfolded before us, my self-centered nature predominated, and this greatly displeased my divine company. I did very little that was not in my own self-interest. Other people's needs were less important than my own desires. This is opposed to the will of God and is the opposite of love.

We watched a student come to me with a serious problem that he was having with a girlfriend. We could hear my thoughts as the student told me his story. I was bored and anxious for the student to leave because I had no interest in his problem. To the student it was of the utmost importance, but it was trivial to me. I gave the student some ill-conceived advice and he left. The angels and Jesus were very disappointed in my failure to care for and communicate with this young man seeking help. God wants us to be compassionate to one another.

We create our eternal judgment by what we do in this world. The truth judges us. In the light of God there is no deception. How many people will cry out to Jesus Christ when they die and be given a life review? He will say to them, "You called me but I never knew you. When did you show compassion to your brother or sister? When did you love me?"

The angels showed me that we do not earn our love of God by the things we do. God's love is given without cost or strings attached. We live lovingly because God loves us so much. Thank God there is a way to change our lives and be forgiven our mistakes.

The next time I leave this world, I will be able to stand with the angels and Jesus Christ and look at my life without constant shame and foreboding of what we will see next.

_____

6

THE PAST AND THE FUTURE

In my conversation with Jesus and the angels, they told me about God. I asked them what God is like and they told me this: God knows everything that will happen and, more important, God knows everything that could happen. From one moment to the next, God is aware of every possible variable of every event and each outcome. God doesn't control or dictate the outcome of every event, which would be a violation of God's creation. This is because every bit of energy and matter has its own integrity and course to fulfill. Every living creature has its own will that must be expressed. Each conscious being has its own learning to be experienced. God created all things to be what they are and knows that the ultimate outcome is part of the Creator's design. Every action serves God's purpose by fulfilling its nature, including the total range of activity from negative to positive. The outcome will always serve God's ultimate purpose, no matter how long or how impossible it appears to us.

Whether we humans understand why things happen or appreciate how things happen is unimportant because we are not in control of creation. Creatures are not the Creator, and this is not our world to control. Our job is to discover how we can be a part of the divine plan. God has given humans a divine image and likeness in order to comprehend our role in the divine plan. God has endowed humans with the divine ability to conceptualize the past and future in order that we may adjust our behavior to further or frustrate the divine will toward ultimate good. God sees our mistakes and allows them to happen knowing we will suffer the consequences of our mistakes. The Supreme Being sees our right decisions and enjoys the knowledge that we have taken another step closer to God.

They explained to me that people experience God's emotions as we participate in the creation just as God participates in the creation and feels our emotions. They told me when we have small children, we make the world around them as safe as possible. We limit the dangers that can harm them. God has done the same by creating a world that has a natural order, that is predictable and very limited in its outcome (our physical universe). The world that we live in and our ability to affect the world is governed by God's design. The principle of cause and effect governs our life experience. God wants us to know this to the very core of our being. Our every thought and every deed has an effect on our sphere of influence. Negative thoughts produce negative actions just as positive thoughts result in positive outcomes.

When I asked why there had been wars, they were quick and emphatic to tell me: "God hates war. God has no desire for you to use violence and destructive means to assert your will over one another. But God allows wars to happen when you are determined to be at war. God has influenced you in the course of your history to find more peaceful methods to resolve your differences. The vast majority of wars that you have desired have not taken place because God subtly influenced people to prevent war. There have been occasions when God has let you suffer the consequences of your desire for war. Every war is a lesson that war is undesirable, and that you need to learn better ways of achieving harmony with one another.

"The two world wars of the twentieth century were not God's will. Those wars were not inevitable or necessary. They happened not because God wanted them, but rather because you wanted them so intensely that you got what you wanted. The two world wars could have been prevented and should never have happened, but there was a conscious desire by enough people wanting to dominate other people that God let you suffer the results of your desire. God suffers every agony that people suffer during war."

I thought: How could we continue to inflict war upon one another if we only knew how much it hurts God?

They responded to my thought. "God wants an end to war, killing, violence, and dominance now. God wanted an end to war thousands of years ago. God is very unhappy with your continuing desire to make wars. God has ensured that every people who tried to assert control over another people has ultimately been defeated. The lessons of war have been completely negative, but people still consider war an option. God wants you to understand the reasons for your differences and to resolve your problems with love and support for one another."

They said, "People have tried to hide their base desire for domination and exploitation through collective pride under the banner of nationalism. This primitive tribal instinct has blinded you from seeing the divine within other people. God loves all people as God's children and wants every one of you to see every person as a child of God. You are to resist and oppose evil in others and in yourselves by every means possible. You are to find ways to resist evil by good means rather than killing. God really meant it when you were told to not kill. And you have been ignoring and deceiving yourselves ever since. Of course, you have a right to defend yourselves and come to the aid of the defenseless. There are alternatives to killing, and God wants you to learn to live in harmony."

I asked again, why then does God allow war to happen? They made it plain to me: "God hates war." If we desire to kill one another, God will not stop us. We are supposed to learn that war is unacceptable and prevent wars from happening. Wars happen because of the spiritual sickness of people. We are to care about all people and be willing to help heal the spiritual sickness before it leads to the desire to kill. The way to prevent war is to love aggressively and care for all people. Sufficient wealth, food, and resources exist for every person in the world. Wars result not because there is a scarcity of resources, but because of our desire to possess the resources to the exclusion of others. God loves every man, woman, and child on this planet more than we love our own children. God wants all people to have food, shelter, meaningful work, and an opportunity to be creative; to learn the truth, have freedom from fear, have self-esteem, be procreative, live in community, find complete joy, trust in God, and become the wonderful people that God created us to be.

Our purpose is to know and do God's will in this life, and we do this when we love one another as God loves us. Every person without exception needs to be loved by us. This is the most difficult and most important lesson of our life. This is what has shaped the past and this is what will create the future. We have failed to learn this fundamental lesson that God has been teaching us from most religious traditions since the beginning of human consciousness. Every religion began with revelations of God, and in time we have perverted these revelations and created religious traditions to serve our worst instincts. God has given us a revelation of God's will to affirm the worth of every individual. When we pervert God's will by constructing religious traditions that demean another people, we have horribly distorted the will of God in order to deny God's will. This grieves God beyond anything else that we do. This is the unforgivable sin against the Holy Spirit. All of heaven is horrified by our use of the name of God to do harm to one another. This is the worst mistake we can make.

I asked how God could let the Holocaust of World War II happen. We were transported to a railway station as a long train of freight cars was being unloaded of its human cargo. The guards were screaming and beating the people into submission. The people were Jewish men, women, and children. Exhausted from hunger and thirst, they were totally disoriented from the ordeal of being rounded up and sent on a long journey to an unknown destination. They believed that they were going to work camps, and that their submission to the brutality of the guards was the only way to survive.

We went to the area where the selection process was taking place and heard the guards talking about "the Angel Maker." We went to the place the guards were referring to as "the Angel Maker," which was a series of ovens. I saw piles of naked corpses being loaded into the ovens, and I began to cry. Jesus said to me, "These are the people God loves." Then he said, "Look up." Rising out of the smoke of the chimneys, I saw hundreds of people being met by thousands of angels taking them up into the sky. There was great joy in the faces of the people, and there appeared to be no trace of a memory of the horrendous suffering they had just endured. How ironic that the guards sarcastically called the ovens "the Angel Maker."

I asked how God could allow this to happen. They told me that this was not God's will. This was an abomination to God. God wants this never to happen again. This was the sacrifice of an innocent people to whom God had given the law to be an example, a light, to the rest of the world. This Holocaust was breaking God's heart. The anguish that Jesus was suffering at the slaughter of his people was too much for me to bear, and I begged that we leave this place. I will never forget this: his anguish at this horror, and what it represents. This was one of the low points in human history.

I asked, Why does God let things like this happen? They told me that God was very unhappy with the course of human history and was going to intervene to change the world. God had watched us sink to depths of depravity and cruelty at the very time that he was giving us the instruments to make the world a godlier world. God had intervened in the world many times before, but this time God was going to change the course of human events. When God had revealed God's own heart and mind by being present to us in the person of Jesus Christ, the world was being consumed by the tyranny of the Roman Empire. The Spirit of God revealed in Jesus Christ defeated the Roman Empire through love. All of the forces of evil that work in the human heart had frustrated the power of the Spirit of Christ. We had regressed back, time after time, to the brutality of the Roman Empire, except that each time we had more God-given knowledge that we had used for destruction. God inspires every insight of science. We had used this inspiration to further our means of destruction. The great gifts that God wants to give us will not be given until we are loving enough to handle them. God wants to give us the power to control matter and energy with our minds, the ability to communicate directly with our thoughts, to travel through time and space by will, to have knowledge by contemplation. The power of these gifts is beyond our wildest imagination, but they will not be ours until we mature spiritually and can use these powers wisely and lovingly.

I asked, "When will this be?" They said the time is coming soon. I informed them that humankind was no better for the lessons of the two world wars and that we were about to have an even worse third world war.

They said, "There will be no more world wars."

I said, "There are forty thousand nuclear weapons aimed and ready to be launched any minute. Someone, somewhere, is going to press the button and there will be a nuclear war."

They said, "No, that is not going to happen. God will not allow a nuclear war."

"Will God reach down and grab the missiles to stop them from exploding?"

"No. God is going to end the Cold War. God loves every creature, and God will not let the world be destroyed by people."

"How is God going to do that?"

"God is changing the hearts of people to love around the world."

"The Cold War won't end for a hundred years," I insisted.

"The Cold War will end in a couple of years."

I was skeptical. "What will come next?"

"The world is at the beginning of a major transformation. It will be a spiritual revolution that will affect every person in the world."

I asked what the world would be like when this change takes place.

We were in a beautiful natural wooded setting. There was no evidence of human intrusion or man-made devices. They told me that this was the future, and that we were in a garden that people tended. People came by and talked with one another. They were dressed simply and wore exotic ornaments. They resembled Native Americans in their dress. I asked what they did. Everyone spent the majority of their time with the children, teaching them about love and the wonders of the natural world. They didn't make any distinction between work and play. They all participated in child-rearing and teaching as the most important activity of their lives. People raised food by sitting next to plants and communing with them. In a few minutes they could harvest mature fruits and vegetables. They ate what they grew immediately, without cooking. The clothing was all made of finely woven fibers. There was very little metal except in the ornaments.

I asked, "Is this paradise?" They laughed and said, "No, only compared to the world you live in. In this future world people will have sickness, but the treatment for disease will always be successful. People will gather around the person in need of help and through prayer, touch, and meditation the disease will be cured. People will grow only enough food for their needs. Collectively, all the people of the world will control the weather. The climate will be regulated by the collective will of humankind. The plants will be loved and raised by individual people. All animals will live in harmony with people. There will be countless small communities of people all over the world and each will have its own identity and culture. There will be many different languages, but all people will be able to communicate telepathically. There will be no technology because there will be no need for devices, since humans will have the power to control matter and energy. People will stay within their communities unless they want to experience life in a culture that has different music, or vegetation, or scientific investigation."

Everybody was a student of nature, which they knew intimately and with which they could communicate, knowing the sensations and vibration of every part of creation. People explored outer space without moving an inch. People communicated telepathically with everyone on Earth and had relationships with intelligent beings on other worlds. There was no space travel because there was no need. People stayed put and shared life experiences across galaxies. People valued the life experience they had been given in this world because they knew it was a precious gift from God. There were no possessions. People sought the welfare of their community in its spiritual health and growth. When someone was troubled, the community focused its attention on that individual. Occasionally an individual would become a recluse for as much time as needed. When a person was satisfied that he had had all the life experience he needed, the community gathered together around him. They had a celebration while such a person lay down and his spirit moved to heaven. This was the cause of great rejoicing. People were born, grew, learned, and died. They lived to love God, love one another, and love themselves.

I was amazed because I thought the future world would look like the science fiction I had been raised on. The future that I was being shown was completely different from what I expected. People lived in extreme simplicity and harmony. There was no want. Everyone was happy. There was no conflict.

I asked, "When will this come about?"

They said, "In two hundred years."

I contradicted them. "Not in two hundred thousand years. People are not ready for this."

They answered, "This is the future that God wants for humanity, and it will happen. This is the world God has created for us to live in. This is the way God created human beings to live."

"How will it happen?" I asked.

They answered, "God is changing the world now. God wants worldwide conversion. God is going to awaken every person to be the person he or she was created to be. Those who accept God's will shall flourish, and those who deny God's love shall perish."

"Will the United States," I asked, "be the leader of the world in this change?"

"The United States has been given the opportunity to be the teacher for the world, but much is expected of those to whom much has been given. The United States has been given more of everything than any country in the history of the world, and it has failed to be generous with its gifts. If the United States continues to exploit the rest of the world by greedily consuming the world's resources, it will have God's blessing withdrawn. Your country will collapse economically, which will result in civil chaos. Because of the greedy nature of people, you will have people killing people for a cup of gasoline. The world will watch in horror as your country is obliterated by strife. The rest of the world will not intervene because they have been victims of your exploitation. They will welcome the annihilation of such selfish people. The United States must change immediately and become the teacher of goodness and generosity to the rest of the world. Today the United States is the primary merchant of war and the culture of violence that you export to the world. This will come to an end because you have the seeds of your own destruction within you. Either you will destroy yourselves or God will bring it to an end if there isn't a change.

"The United States has been given the opportunity to be the peacemaker of the world. With its medical, agricultural, manufacturing, and scientific knowledge, America could teach less fortunate countries how to give every person food, clothing, housing, medical care, education, and economic prosperity. The United States has the power to help every person in the world access clean water and hygienic waste disposal. Millions of people in the world are dying for lack of things that people in the United States take for granted. This is not God's will. God wants you to know that every person is your brother and sister. God wants every person to have the same chance for fulfillment that a person in America has. God sees the people of the United States becoming increasingly greedy, self-centered, and uncaring. There must be a turning to God, or the reign of the United States will end."

Since 1985, when I was told these things about the future, the Cold War ended with little bloodshed. There have been signs of a great spiritual awakening taking place worldwide. Interest in God, religion, life after death, and personal spirituality has grown dramatically. The self-centeredness of American culture hasn't changed appreciably, which is cause for grave concern. I don't know if the richest country in the history of the world is doomed to lose God's blessing or if the people of the United States will become the moral light of the world. How long will God allow the injustice to continue? The future lies in the choices we make right now. God is intervening in direct ways in human events. May God's will be done on earth as it is in heaven.

7

WHAT HAPPENS WHEN WE DIE

I asked, "What happens when we die?" The following is the answer.

When people die, they don't know that they have died. The world looks the same to them, and they feel completely alive. Whatever trauma a person experienced in dying is only a vivid memory. The suffering is gone and the person feels physically better than he or she ever did in life.

There is disturbing confusion, however, because the individual cannot interact with other people or his surroundings. No one can hear or see him. Nothing responds to her touch.

Most people are not ready to die and can't accept the fact they have died. Some people are ready and are relaxed and eagerly anticipate the reunion with loved ones who have preceded them. This is the condition that makes their transition beautiful and advances them toward heaven.

After death, you will be receptive to God's love or you will not, depending on how you have lived your life. Only God knows what is in a person's heart. How we judge people has little to do with how God knows us. We judge people by their actions, and God knows us by our intentions. God knows every deed, every thought, and every motivation that we have. If we have loved God, loved the one that God has sent to us, loved our fellow person, and loved ourselves, we are drawn toward God. If we have not loved God, God's Son, our fellow person, or ourselves, we are repulsed by God's love. There is nothing in between. Every person knows inside whether or not he or she has lived lovingly. God knows.

❧

The love of God, the love of neighbor, and the love of self are inseparable parts of a whole that cannot be divided. Without the love of God, there cannot be true love of another. It is only through the overarching Spirit of God that one can love another person. Love comes from God, and relationships not grounded in the love of God are based on the exploitation of other people. Only through the love of God can we see the true value and beauty of another person.

It is impossible to love another person unless we love ourselves. Without the love of God, it is impossible to love ourselves because every human being is aware of their flawed nature and sinfulness. We can find ourselves truly lovable only by receiving the love that our Creator has for us. When there is no love of God, there is only the counterfeit love of narcissism, which is a gross attempt to prove ourselves lovable. The only authentic love in this world is achieved when there is a balance between love of God, love of neighbor, and love of self.

Our lives are our judgment. God doesn't need witnesses, arguments, juries, and testimony to know the truth of our lives. The Spirit of God that lives with us is the spirit of truth, and this spirit is the eyes and ears of God. Even if we are blinded by self-deception, the spirit knows the truth because it is truth.

A person who loves God knows he or she is utterly dependent on God's love and mercy. A person who loves God knows that we were created to be the children of God and that we have all failed to be and to live the way God created us. A person who loves God knows that it is only because of and through the great love of God that we are raised up from death into new life. Only a person who loves God can accept that God would suffer and die for us so that we may be raised up to life with God. God defeated the power of death through God's great love for us. Jesus is God's redemptive act for a fallen world.

❦

When a loving person dies, God sends angels to escort them on their journey to heaven. Angels are the messengers of God. They could be relatives or friends, but they will be exactly the right persons who represent God's love to the individual. The persons you long for, who have gone to heaven before you, will be waiting for you when you die. They will be ready to comfort you and escort you to heaven.

They will take you from the reality of this physical universe and transport you to a new reality where you get your first introduction to the wonder and power of God. There are as many entry points into heaven as there are individuals. Each person is escorted toward heaven according to his or her life, culture, and spiritual level. One person may be in a beautiful field, another may be in a magnificent castle, another in a setting similar to their grandparents' home. God and the angels, for the specific comfort and beginning edification of that person, individually create each setting. It is difficult for us to understand and believe how much God cares about and respects our individuality.

The angel guardians begin the process of explaining to the person that they have left the world and are beginning life. Everything behind was preparation for real life. What we call death is actually being born into a new life beyond our imagination. We will grow and be transformed. We will meet the personification of God, and eventually we will come before the very presence of God.

❦

This is what they said happens to a person who has hated God in this life. If a person is not ruled by the love of God, he or she is ruled by hatred of God. The greatest hatred of God is to be indifferent to God. We were created and put in this world to know God's will and to live accordingly. To disregard this is contempt for the God of the Universe. A person who is indifferent to God is repelled by His light and love.

Every person has guardian angels all their lives throughout his or her life. Our angels are the embodiment of compassion for us. Because of their reverence for God, they cannot impose themselves on us or intervene in our lives when we choose to reject them and God's love. The more we despise our angels, the more we are on our own. Our desire for self-sufficiency insulates us from the divine order for our lives. When we realize our need for God and God's messengers, we grow in desire and opportunity to live in the divine order. Love attracts more love and hate attracts hate.

A person devoid of the love of God cannot be welcomed into the journey to heaven. They are left on their own.

They are not alone in life after death. They have kindred

spirits, people like them who are waiting for them. These kindred spirits are their welcoming committee, which takes them on a journey away from the love and light of God. For every individual there is a unique journey into the abyss. There is no limit to its complexity and depths of distress. On this journey a person embarks on an unending life without God. Hell is separation from God.

♦

Everything good comes from God. Life without God is when every good thing does not exist. There is no love, no light, no hope, no joy, no compassion, no truth, and no peace without God. This is a reality of hate, darkness, despair, suffering, cruelty, lies, and fighting. How it is experienced is proportionate to the life of the individual. God will not intervene, and the angels cannot intervene because this has been the individual's choice. God respects our freedom to choose.

For some people this may culminate in the ultimate annihilation of their being, if after they have existed in this eternity they still do not seek their way back to God. For others there is the possibility of salvation. In the Christian tradition, Jesus Christ journeyed into the depths of hell and saved lost souls. This could happen again. But the terrible truth is that the deeper people sink into degradation, the less willing they are to seek salvation. Many desire annihilation as relief from the torment of hell.

God loves *all* people and doesn't desire one to withdraw into the darkness. God has emotions, and God suffers, when one soul is lost to the darkness. The angels suffered just telling me about those who reject God's love. They couldn't bear the thought of God's misery when one person is lost in hell.

Even though God does not want one person to go to hell,

God will not stop a person who is determined to go there. Whether we go to heaven or hell is determined by the choice we make. Do we accept God or not? If a person doesn't know the answer to that question, he has rejected God.

❦

I don't like to talk about the place of eternal torment because of my own painful experience there. God and God's messengers don't want to talk about such a hideous place of suffering. God wants to draw us to heaven through love, not fear of punishment. There are two kinds of fear of God. One is the acknowledgment that God is God and we are powerless, or nothing, without God. This fear is awe, or reverence, for God, and it leads us to surrender to and receive God's love, which always leads to our love for God. The other kind of fear of God is to be afraid of God and to reject God's love. Why do we do this? I don't know the answer. I only know it breaks God's heart every time a person does it. Those who have accepted God's love not only make God happy, they make all of heaven joyous. It is difficult to imagine with our limited understanding, but the truth is that heaven rejoices every time a person makes the decision to love God and live according to God's will.

After we have chosen God, the greatest joy in the world is to help another person to accept God. God wants us to be fully alive, utterly happy. Our distinct personalities and gifts as an individual are what God loves. Just as we choose to love a life mate because of his or her own unique character, so God created us and chooses us because of our uniqueness.

When we journey to heaven, the very best of who we are is increased and amplified, and the deficiencies in our character are washed away. We have to be willing to let go of our mistakes and eager to develop our gifts. We are not alone in this process of purification. All of heaven conspires to help us become perfect sons and daughters of God.

Everyone begins their journey toward God in their own way according to their spiritual need. The paths are unlimited and the end is the same, which is God. Those who have been in the presence of God, who is the center of heaven, return to the source of being frequently. Those who have been with God take God's Spirit with them wherever they go. We were made in the image and likeness of God. We are God's children, so we return to our source. God is the ultimate reality, and we find our completeness, our wholeness in God. We find that our journey toward God is the sole and entire reason for our very being. We desire nothing other than to be reunited with the One, the cause of all that is.

Everything we lack we are supplied, and everything that is an impediment we release. All of our questions are answered. We do not leave this world spiritually ready to meet God in person, so God brings us to God's self in stages.

In our progression toward God we will meet the Divine Activity of God, who is known to Christians as Jesus Christ. People who were not Christians must know the Christ as well. No one approaches God who does not know the mediator of God. The Christ is the creative action by which the world was created. This personification of God has been everywhere throughout all time and space—creating, restoring, and sustaining us in the divine will. The Christ has been in our world and adopted our human nature to help return us to God. The Christ, in the man Jesus of Nazareth, lived, suffered, died, and was raised to new life to restore us to God. He has identified with us so that we can identify with him. Jesus Christ took upon himself all of our failings so that we can become complete, whole, and perfect, as he is perfect. He has the power and the desire to make us perfect. We do not have that power, but when we want to be perfect, he will make us like him in perfect love of God.

Gradually, in just the right increments, we become like him, while we retain our identity and unique qualities. What separates us from God is our own sense of separateness. What unites us with God is awareness of our oneness with God. We have learned our separateness through experience, and we will learn our oneness only through the same process. As God experienced separateness dying on a cross in front of a jeering crowd, we will learn our Christ nature in the arms of the saints guiding us through the journey into the light of God.

Anything good is possible on this journey to God. The universe is full of worlds, many far superior to the one we left. We might visit or choose a life in a better world in preparation for our union with God. Some people have left behind loved ones that need their protection and guidance. They can live as guardian angels for a while as part of their spiritual development. Some apprentice themselves to great angels to learn lessons they missed in this life. Anything good is possible. The universe and heaven are full of life experiences to teach us about God. Some people need time to contemplate, some need activity, and they are all on the spiritual journey. The universe is more varied and full of life than we can imagine. All of this richness of experience can be a growing experience to becoming Christlike, to be united with God.

In the center of heaven is the One God surrounded by a vast number of beings that have achieved divinity as the children of God. None of them dream for a moment that they are God. They retain their identity united in God. They participate with God in creation.

The universe exists because it is the activity of God and the heavenly multitude. It was explained to me that it is like a vast orchestra and God is the conductor. Each individual is an instrument with unique qualities. Each soul contributes in their unique way to the symphony of creation. There is no past or future in the symphony, only present. The universe and all that is in it is the music. We are the songs sung by heaven. Outside of this symphony of life there is no time, space, matter, or energy. Within the heavenly orchestra are all time, space, matter, and energy. Our ultimate destiny is to participate with God in creation. The instrument we play is our being perfectly connected to God by the bond of love. We know our part in the symphony because we have understood who we are and contribute our experience, our whole being, our spirit into the process.

No one makes a mistake. That is why the preparation is so extensive and arduous. Everyone is perfect because they are perfectly connected to the conductor. It is no coincidence that music is called the universal language and used as a form of worship. All of God's children have a place in the choir. The heavenly host resides around God in adoration, actively giving praise by giving one's whole self to God.

This is perfect ecstasy.

❧

When we attempt to imagine what this must be like, we know deep inside we are not ready. But through the transformative power of Christ, we will be made ready in God's time.

The popular images of heaven that exist today are ridiculous compared to the truth about heaven that I was shown. Everything good that was is in heaven in some form. Everyone in heaven is in immortal form so there is no need for any material thing. Everyone in heaven is on a spiritual journey. Sitting by the ocean watching the rhythm of the waves, reading a book written by an ancient wise man, talking with a saint, embracing a loved one reunited for the first time after a long absence all reflect life in heaven. Talking with the Christ about his life as Jesus and asking him every question and his wonderful answers are some of the joys of heaven.

There is no urgency or anxiety about anything. We move at our own pace, acquiring the wholeness we lack and relieving ourselves of our doubts and deficiencies.

As we grow in our Christ nature, we become physically changed. We gradually lose our opaqueness and become translucent. Our bodies become radiant and we are able to open ourselves to the radiance of others. We give our light and receive the light of others. Communication is an exchange of thought, feelings, and love of such intimacy and intensity that it can't be described. Souls meet and join together. Everything in heaven is good, so there is never any fear, suffering, or anger. People in heaven can look back into the world they left and see exactly what is happening. They know that in spite of appearances, God's perfect plan is unfolding in the lives of the people they have left behind.

Heaven looks upon this world and prays to God to help us come into the light and love of God. Those who have gone to heaven before us look upon us, praying we will make the right choices. They know the grief we experience because they are gone from us. They also know that separation is only for a few moments, and then we will be reunited forever. They want us to make the most of the lives that we have been given so that we will join them in heaven. The reunions that take place in heaven are so joyful. Our lives in the world are very brief, and if we are fully engaged in life, the time passes quickly. The embrace of families and old friends makes the pain of absence disappear immediately and instead there is eternal joy.

This life that God has given us is a precious gift. We are to use it wisely because this opportunity to prepare ourselves for heaven is given only once. No one will ever be given this exact opportunity again. God does not bestow the gift of life on us frivolously or arbitrarily. We are given this life opportunity to prepare ourselves for our continuing spiritual growth in heaven. Failing to use our life opportunities wisely and lovingly is a rejection of God. Throwing one's life away is a rejection of God and is not preparation for heaven. The choices we make in this world determine whether we are candidates for heaven or not. In each of us we know whether we are going to heaven or not. If you don't know the answer, you are in big trouble and need to ask God to show you the way immediately. Fortunately, God wants us to come HOME, and God has sent us someone to show us the way home. His name is Jesus.

8

WHY WE ARE THE WAY WE ARE

When I asked the angels and Jesus why we are the way we are, we had a long conversation about human nature. If I were to summarize everything in one sentence, it is this: God loves us very much. This is the essence of what I learned and what I want to communicate from my experience. This seems so simple, but it has tremendous implications.

Being children of God has benefits and responsibilities. The single most important fact of being God's children is knowing that God loves us. God's love has no parallel in human experience. God is self-sufficient and doesn't need anything. Humans are totally dependent on God and we are extremely needy people. How can we compare the love of the Creator who loves unconditionally with the love of the created who loves conditionally. This is the dilemma: trying to understand God's love for us, and why we are the way we are.

We have no basis for knowing unconditional love. Anyone who has had an experience of God's love knows it is ineffable. God's love is beyond our ability to describe or to even conceptualize. Imagine what it would be like to compress every feeling of love from your entire life into one intense moment of love. God's love for us is still greater.

If you want a glimpse of God's love, look at a mother nursing her baby. This is as close to the love of God as we will know in this world. It is no coincidence that the image of a mother nursing her baby is one of the most often depicted images in Christian art. God is like a mother and father to us. We are completely dependent on God like the baby is dependent on its parents. To think we are self-sufficient is what separates us from God. This delusion of independence is pride, and pride is the source of all sin (that which intentionally separates us from God).

To know God's love, we have to rid ourselves of the delusion of independence. We create our ego in response to the experience of our life. Tragically, we create egos that eliminate our relationship with God. Even people who think they are religious often attempt to manipulate God for their own self-centered purposes. This is one of the greatest travesties that we commit against God—to project our mean spirit onto God. God's love for all people is the foundation for the beginning of knowing something about God's love.

The egocentric view of God is often projected into a tribal view of God's love. God is not confined to individuals, tribes, nations, religions, or any other institutions. Our cultural bias is collective egocentric pride. Since we are finite creatures raised in specific cultures, we are shaped by our culture. To know God, we have to surrender our individual and collective pride/ego if we are ever to know God's love.

Too often we claim God's love for our closed group. We exclude everyone outside the group as being outside God's love.

This is opposed to God's will. God loves everyone beyond anything we can imagine. God loves atheists, agnostics, murderers, prostitutes, thieves, drunks, drug addicts, homeless people, and liars. God abhors behavior that demeans and destroys godliness, but God loves the person.

A parent may raise a child who becomes a criminal, but the parent loves the son or daughter and hates the behavior of the offspring. God loves us whatever we do, but God does not like the evil we do.

God's love allows us to do anything we want to do. The things we do can give God joy or they can hurt God, and God watches over us, loves us, and tries to influence us to be godly people. God doesn't control us. God could control us, but it is the nature of God's love to let us reap the consequences of our actions.

The angels and Jesus explained it to me this way: God's love is like a family. When a child is born, the parents make the home as safe as possible to protect the baby. They attend to every need of the baby. As the baby becomes an infant, the parents keep it from harm and try to teach it to be aware of the needs of others. As the infant grows and becomes an adolescent, the parents struggle to impose safe limitations on the child's exposure to danger and provide it with significant life experiences to equip it for independent adulthood. Most parents have wished they could keep their child safe from harm forever. The parent knows that to love your children, you can only equip them for life and then out of love let them go. Parents can never stop loving their child no matter what happens. The child becomes an adolescent and an adult capable of pleasing the parents or disappointing them. The parents try to influence but not control what their mature children do.

God has created a world where we are treated like mature children of God. God influences us but doesn't control our behavior. The rain falls on the just and the unjust equally.

God holds us individually and collectively responsible for our actions. God influences our goodness with blessings and discourages our evil with withdrawal of blessings. God's blessings are spiritual. Love, hope, faith, and peace are the blessings God gives as encouragement for godly living. Hate, despair, unbelief, and strife are the result of turning away from God. Wealth, power, and status are unimportant to God. These are distractions from the purpose of our lives. Each of us is to use the wealth, power, and status that we have attained for the reign of God's love in the world as it is in heaven.

God's justice is that we will all reap the consequences of our actions in this world and in the next life.

Some people are moving toward God's blessing, which is bliss. Some people are heading toward torment. God wants all people to come to heaven, but God allows each of us to choose between bliss and torment, heaven or hell. In this world we can mix bliss and torment. In the next life heaven and hell are separated.

The angels and Jesus told me that God doesn't want anyone to go to the place of torment. Why would anyone choose hell? Why do people make their lives in this world hell? Why do people reject God? Why do people hate one another? The answer is, because we can. God gave us the godlike ability to create and destroy. God has given us the godlike capacity to become saints or demons. God has equipped us to become whatever we choose.

My heavenly teachers stated that we cannot say we don't know the difference. Every person has sufficient spiritual insight to know the difference. We also have an unlimited capacity for self-deception. The bad claim they are good, and the good think they are bad. In our hearts we know what we are. God is not deceived. God knows exactly whether love or hate rules us. Those ruled by love go toward God, to heaven. Those ruled by hate go to hell. Our lives are the judge. We create our own fate in the next life. What happens to people as they leave this world and enter eternity is between them and God. If they have striven to love God, they are drawn to God. If they hate God, they are drawn away from God. It is too wonderful and too terrible to speculate further. We all know in our hearts where we are going in the next life. We know what we must do to change our destiny. Are we willing to make the change?

God doesn't want anyone to go away from God. In this world and in the next, God calls all people. No one is good enough to go to heaven, yet God wants all of us to go to heaven. We choose between God and separation from God. God's love has given us the freedom and ability to choose. God's love will allow the greatest sinner in the world to choose heaven. God will allow the kindest person to go to hell. As we live in God's love or opposed to God's love, we are making our choice. The evidence of how we express God's love is how we love one another. Jesus commanded his disciples to love one another. This is the way to heaven. The opposite is the path to hell. It's not complicated. We know in our hearts where we are going. Heaven is a gift from God we don't deserve, except for God's love for us. Hell is what we desire when we reject God.

Our perspective on life is wrong. We think this life in the world is important. It is only important as preparation for our eternal life. The only importance of this life is the choice we make to love God or not. When we die, our souls leave this world and move into a different dimension or new reality. What we have chosen determines whether that will be a reality of bliss or torment. Everything we do in life is a result of the choice we have made. We are either moving toward God or away from God. There is nothing in between. You cannot be neutral about God. To be indecisive about God is opposition to God. The Creator of the Universe, Supreme Being, Highest Lord, is not something one can ignore.

When we feel love toward another person, we know it. When we don't feel love for another person, we know it. The opposite of love is indifference. The opposite of the love of God is indifference to God. This is pure hate. To reject God so completely as to be indifferent is the most opposed to God we can be. To be angry with God is different. When we are in a loving relationship, we feel all emotions intensely. We can scream in anger, "My God, my God, why have you abandoned me?" We can wrestle, argue, plead, laugh, cry, hold, and push away the person we are in love with.

Love is an intense, caring relationship that elicits powerful emotions. God invites us into an intimate and intense relationship. God wants to be reconciled to us. The Book of Psalms expresses every conceivable emotion toward God. These songs are prayer, praise, and laments to God.

God wants us to be happy. Doesn't every good father and mother want their child to be happy? God wants the same for the children of God. God gives us this little life in the world for us to choose whether we will be with God forever or whether we will move away from God in the next life. This life is very brief, and when we go to eternity we will understand how very brief our time in the world really was. We are each given precisely enough life to make our choice.

I was told that questions and doubts are the means to discover the truth. God gave us the power of reason to examine, question, and test the validity of our thoughts. "Then why do we become plagued with doubts and indecision?" I asked. They told me that I had chosen indecision as my means to avoid making a choice. This is not an option when it comes to the most critical decision of life, whether to love God or not.

We maintain our indifference to God by wallowing in doubt. By perpetually doubting God, we are negating God. Can we doubt whether our mother or father exists? Do we doubt that we owe them some gratitude and respect for giving us birth and raising us? Doubting God is a rejection of our Creator and the One who loves us.

No one ever born was good enough to go to heaven. God made us incomplete so that we would become perfect through our love for God. If we were perfect, we wouldn't have any need for God. We are not gods. We have God in us and with us, but we are far from being God. God knows our deficiency and has done something to bring us home to perfection.

God has sent teachers and prophets into the world to show us the way to heaven. There have been thousands of teachers all over the world. There have been many prophets all over the world. These have been men and women sent and inspired by God's Spirit to show us the way. People have ignored the teachers and prophets and perverted their message.

God came into the world by filling a man with the Spirit of God. This man was human in every way and the perfect love, will, and Spirit of God in every way. Incredibly, this person came via the most humble, impoverished birth imaginable. His infancy was spent as a refugee. His youth and early adulthood were spent as a skilled craftsman. He lived in an occupied and oppressed country far from the center of power of the civilized world. He taught and healed the sick for three years and was killed, suffering the worst possible death of a criminal. After he was dead and buried, he reappeared many times to hundreds of people. By his death, he conquered the power of death and invited all people to eternal life with God in heaven.

The reason he has a billion and a half followers today is because he is alive, speaks, and heals today. This man from God was named Jesus of Nazareth, and his followers called him the Chosen One, the Christ. He offers all people forgiveness of their sins and eternal life in heaven. By his life and self-sacrifice, he has done for us what we could never do. He has made us perfect, complete, and at one with God. When we trust him, he will raise us up to heaven.

Jesus said, "I am the Resurrection and the life. Those who trust me, even though they die, will live." Whether people claim they are Christians or not is not what is ultimately important. What is important is whether one loves as he loved. This is loving with the unconditional love of God. A person can love God and love his brother and sister unconditionally without being a Christian. Calling oneself a Christian doesn't make one a follower of Jesus Christ if one doesn't love as he loved.

Jesus said, "I am the way, and the truth, and the life. No one comes to the Father except through me." No one will go to God except through the atonement of Christ, the love of Christ, and the way of Christ. Jesus' teachings and practice were inclusive of all people. Humans have tried to make him into an exclusive cult, but Jesus came for all people, and the Christ reaches to all people everywhere in all time, space, heaven, and hell. In my experience I was with him, and I will never be apart from him in this world or the next. During my time with Jesus, I discovered he is my best friend. I love him.

9

REALITY

D uring my Near-Death Experience, I was given the opportunity to ask Jesus and the angels a variety of questions. Here are some of the answers they gave.

❦

Question: Where did the creation come from?
There was never time, space, or matter before God. The angels refer to God in many ways, but the term most often used is The One. God is The One because God is the source of everything. There is NO THING other than God. Everything came from God and everything returns to God.

They explained to me in a way I could understand that God is like an artist who creates for the sheer pleasure of creating. One of our attributes that is in the image and likeness of God is our desire to create. We are creative not only as artists, musicians, writers, and performers, but as parents, workers, healers, lovers, and learners.

God creates universes, which in turn became procreative.

There are countless intelligent beings in the universe we inhabit and infinitely more in universes that occupy other dimensions. God is present to all the creation.

The creation is entirely in the *now* to God. God's consciousness is the entire creation. Everything that was, and everything that will be, is *this moment* to God. Our understanding of past and future, space and separateness, is not how God comprehends creation. God is incomprehensible to us except in the ways that he has chosen to reveal the true nature of himself to us. We have been given the ability to know God by being made in "the image and likeness of God." The prime characteristic that allows us to know something about God is love. Love is to care intensely about something. We say we love chocolate, fishing, history, a person, cars, gardening, flying, sewing, music, and so on. The passion we experience is sharing in God's passion for everything. Our love is from God. When we love, we experience God. God loves everything passionately. Love is infinitely complex because there are so many variables. We were created to learn how to love. It takes more than a lifetime of experience to learn how to live lovingly. Every person will be given all the experiences one needs to learn how to love.

❧

Question: Are we physical or spirit?
We are the projected children of the mind of God, the Spirit made flesh. We are the expression of the Spirit and ultimately co-participants of creation in an ever-increasing, ever-expanding, ever-diversified, unceasing continuum. God can create infinitely. How does God create divine Spirit in infinite varieties that have never existed and are beyond manipulation? If you make a piece

of art of any inanimate object, it just sits there; it doesn't have any life. But if you give birth to a child, the child develops a life of its own. It becomes different from you. God has created a universe that not only has sufficient energy, but that also is becoming infinitely more complex every single moment, richer and more varied in terms of Spirit, experience, emotion, and thought. God is enjoying being every one of God's creations. God delights in every created being thinking about God. Imagine contemplating yourself from all the points of view of everyone in the universe. It's God being God through God's creation.

Matter is a state of energy. Energy is a realization of the divine mind. Energy is created in a vibration of the divine mind. It takes time and planning to get energy to a point where it can be brought to a more sophisticated and structured state, which is matter. It takes more time and planning to get matter to a point where matter can produce life.

❖

Question: Who manages all of this?
Many of the angels are involved in the organization of the physical universe. They cause these events to happen; they develop matter through its stages of evolution. There is God's mind and will behind everything that happens. There is a great deal of intelligence and will bringing the world into being. It is ongoing every moment.

The function of the angels in relation to the evolution of the earth is a lot like gardening, with a gentle touch. You plant the seed, you water it, you prune the plant, you tend it, but it has a life of its own. Anyone who gardens knows that the more in tune you are in allowing the thing to be what it can become, rather than forcing it, the more effective you are in helping it develop to its full potential.

❦

Question: What is the goal of life's evolution?
Everything is a manifestation of God's mind and God's will.
Living things as opposed to inanimate objects have more of God's
will in them. There is an obvious difference between a plant and
a stone. A stone is an emanation from God, but a plant has the
ability to turn, to grow, to move, to reproduce itself. A highly active being, such as an animal, is as different from a plant as a
plant is from a stone. Reasoning beings are as different from non-
reasoning beings as animals are from plants.

The divine Spirit that causes beings to be born is very, very
special. There is something very wonderful going on in a human
baby, in the joining of the male and female that makes a fetus.
That little divine sparkle is the spiritual germ of what will develop into a fully developed soul. It's the potential, which
through the course of human development can become a mature
soul, ready to evolve into pure Spirit.

If a baby dies, its soul goes back to the source. Inside the
bulb of a tulip is the tulip plant. In the spore of a fern is the
whole fern. Everything that fern can be is there. This is the case
with the human fetus. To become fully developed as a mature
soul, it all has to live experientially.

When an adult dies, this person may have fully fulfilled all
that could be learned in the physical. Any more would be redun-
dancy. One doesn't learn it all perfectly, but that final honing and
polishing of the spirit will be accomplished outside of the physical. We are shaped to develop as spiritual beings.

A child is full of potential; it hasn't become the full instrument, the complete, unique, individual, developed, willful, intelligent, spiritual instrument of God. If the soul fails in the

physical, for whatever reasons, it will go back to the source. It may come back into this physical world or another. Were it to come back, which is just one of countless possibilities, it would be more highly developed.

The important thing is to realize one's potential here and now. We are not to rely on a desire to escape from one's responsibilities of being God's people, here and now.

Each moment of our life in this world is the critical opportunity to say "Yes" to God. This is the moment to trust God. This is the day to respond to God's love. We respond to God's love by re-creating ourselves in the image and likeness of God. This is not difficult to discover because God has given us a perfect model to instruct us in perfect love. He lived two thousand years ago, and he lives today. He will send his Spirit into our lives if we ask him. His spirit, which is the Spirit of Christ, will guide us and reveal God's nature to us as we become spiritual beings. All we have to do is invite the Spirit of Christ Jesus into our lives and we have begun our journey to heaven.

❦

Question: What is reality?
My experience with heaven and hell showed me that there is a vastly greater reality than what I had previously known. The religious mysteries direct us toward the true nature of reality that we are unaware of. Religion opens our mind and spirit to the greater reality. When we face the mysteries of our existence, we can surrender our ego and begin to experience more of the greater reality. Much of what has been called supernatural is only what we don't understand.

❦

Question: Which is the best religion?

I was expecting them to answer with something like Methodist or Presbyterian or Catholic, or some other denomination.

They answered, "The religion that brings you closest to God."

❧

Question: But which one is that?

There are good people in bad religions and there are bad people in good religions. It is not so important which religion, but what individuals do with the religion they have been given. Religions are a vehicle to take you to a destination. The purpose of religion is to help you have a personal relationship with God. God wants us to love him with all our being and to know the truth of God. If we find God in an intimate, loving relationship, then we are going the right way. Too often people find religion to be self-serving, interested in perpetuating itself and controlling people's lives in order to be dominant. Religion is only a means to find God. Religion is not the destination. True religion is the love of God in every word, thought, and deed of the person. God loves all people and is pleased by religions that seek him in spirit and in truth.

God abhors the misuse of religion that creates divisiveness between people, that justifies violence, that promotes pride in self-righteousness. God is far greater than any religion. The Spirit of Christ speaks to all people in all time to draw them to God.

❧

Question: What about atheism?

There is no such thing as atheism. It is impossible to believe in nothing. God is the source of everything, so to say that you don't

believe in God is just foolishness. People who say they don't believe in God are really saying that they are angry with God or that
they don't believe in the image of God they were told to believe
in. If you exist, you believe in God. If you think, you believe in
God. People are incapable of knowing or having any understanding of God without God's self-revelation. God has revealed the
true nature of himself to many people. Anyone who desires to
know God will have God revealed.

❧

Question: Is Jesus the Son of God?
Jesus said, "Yes."

God came into the experience of human life through him.
God's spirit was so complete in the human person of Jesus that
he was God with us.

❧

*Question: Why did he not do something spectacular to prove it to
everyone?*
God wants us to choose God freely, without coercion. God doesn't
threaten or need to force our belief. God wants our love and trust,
for love alone. God doesn't want slaves in mindless obedience.
God wants us to choose God freely. Behavior that looks religious
but is devoid of genuine love is abhorrent to God. God loves an
honest agnostic more than a religious hypocrite.

❧

*Question: I asked Jesus: Are the things written about him in the Bible
true?*
He said that the stories in the Bible about Jesus are only a small
sample of who he is and what he has done. All the books in the

world couldn't contain what he has done. The stories about him in the Bible are sufficient for us to know him and what he represents. He is the revelation of the unknowable God. That is what he wants us to know. He has spoken to many people in many times, millions upon millions throughout time in our world, so that people would know the intimate, personal love of God.

❧

Question: Why did Jesus have to put up with our rejection of him and be treated the way he was?

He said, "I came to accept you as you are. In my love there was no barrier or limit. I embraced you and everything that you are—both love and hate, good and evil."

Through his brief life with us, we know that nothing can separate us from the love of God. Nothing we do can separate us from God unless we want this. No matter what we have said or done, God is willing, eager, and begging us to turn back to God. Even if we think we have nailed God to a tree, God looks into our eyes and says, "I forgive you because you do not know what you are doing."

The love of Jesus is without recrimination. When we ask him to forgive us the mistakes and insults we have done to him, he has already forgiven us. We cannot hurt him except by rejecting him. We can't shock him or surprise him because he already knows. He is the best friend anyone could possibly ever have because he knows us and loves us exactly the way we are and only wants what is best for us. He doesn't tell us that we must change in order for him to accept us. He loves us just as we are, and we beg him to help us change so that we may be worthy of his love.

❧

Question: What about people who use his name to teach hatred?
He was very clear that they would regret that they had done that.
He will reject from his presence anyone who uses his name to
promote hatred. Using the name of God or the name of Jesus
Christ to serve one's own purpose is an unforgivable insult to the
spirit of truth.

❦

*Question: I asked Jesus: Has he been to another world besides my
world?*
He said he had been to every world in every time and space. He
said that he had brought the revelation of God to all intelligent
beings. Some beings had been as stubborn as we were to accept
him, and many more worlds had gladly accepted him. He said
he would come back to our world in good time when we were
ready to accept him.

10

THE ARGUMENT

I asked every question I could think of to ask, and they answered every one. They told me that I needed to return to the world. What a shock, since I was hoping that we would continue our journey to heaven. Jesus would make me perfect and I would join the saints in my spiritual journey to God. Although I was painfully aware of my imperfection, I knew that Jesus could remove my deficiencies by filling me with his love and knowledge.

"I can't go back to the world. The world is full of evil and ugliness," I protested.

"The world has evil and ugliness in it, but there is also ample goodness, love, and beauty if you seek it," they responded.

"But I saw mostly the bad in people and the cruel things they do to each other."

"You will find what you look for in people and in the world. If you are loving, you will find love. If you seek beauty, you will see beauty. If you pursue goodness, you will receive goodness. What you are inside will attract the same from outside. When you love, love comes to you. When you hate, hate finds you."

"Sometimes people love and they receive hate in return," I argued.

"Love is more powerful than hate and love always wins."

"But good people are killed by evil people."

"How you judge the outcome is not how things really are. You judge by appearances. That is not the reality of how things really are. You think wealth, possessions, physical attractiveness, and long life are success in life. They don't necessarily mean anything. Some of the people God has favored with the gifts of love, wisdom, joy, and hope never had wealth, power, material things, physical beauty, or long lives. When God came into the world through Jesus, he had none of these things. They are insignificant compared to the spiritual growth of the soul. Life in the world is not about acquisitions, power, or pleasure. You are given a life in the world for only one purpose, which is to love God. You love God by learning God's will and doing God's will by loving one another. Anything else is immaterial to the purpose of your brief life experience in the world."

"How could I know God's will?" I asked.

"God has sent many teachers into the world to teach the message that you are to love one another. God has clearly demonstrated this message by Jesus' life in the world and by the countless examples of people who have known God's love and shared that love with their brothers and sisters. In the center of every soul is the love of God and the desire to receive God's love and share that love with all of God's children. To realize who you truly are and to become a child of God is the only reason you were born into the world."

"But why don't we know that?"

"You have been given the greatest gift God gives to his people. The ability to accept God's love or refuse it is the greatest freedom and the attribute God gives to any person. God will not force love on anyone. True love has to be freely given and freely received. Love has no strings attached. You live in the world to learn the true nature of love. Have no expectation of reward for loving. Have no assurance of benefit other than becoming part of God's love."

"Why doesn't God do something to get people's attention? Why doesn't God turn the sky red-orange and write in the clouds, 'LOVE GOD'? Why doesn't God do something so spectacular that we would know what we are supposed to do?"

"God will not demand your love. That defeats the very nature of love. Love must be a choice. You cannot scare people into loving. That is not love, it is submission. God doesn't want slaves. God wants people to freely choose love. You know very well that you have been free to choose to receive or reject God's love. Every person ever born has had the same opportunity. Every person has struggled with the same choice."

"Why is it easier for some than others? How can a person choose God's love when they live in a horrible environment?"

"The environment that a person is born into is the people who nurture goodness and love, or the people who teach hate and distrust. The environment is not material. Loving people come out of the worst slums in the world and hateful people grow up in the richest homes. Each soul is free to choose, and the circumstances of their culture can influence them, but they do not determine what a person will choose. Even the best of circumstances with the most loving parents can produce a person who rejects love, and the worst environment with the cruelest of parents can produce a loving person. It is between the individual and God whether they have a loving relationship, and every person is free to choose no matter what anyone does. People will always be free to reject God because God has given you that gift of freedom. You need to understand that God has given you the greatest gift God can give to any creature: to become part of God's love or to not become part of God's love."

"Why did I choose to reject God's love?"

"You know the answer to that already. You were angry with the people in authority over your life. You were angry at everything you thought they believed in. You tried to re-create yourself in the image of a person self-sufficient from the people around you. You wanted to be the only center of your universe. You would be the measure of all things. You tried to become your own god. Look at how well that worked for you."

"But if I go back into the world I will make mistakes, like I did before. Maybe I will make the same mistakes. I can't go back knowing that I will choose to separate myself from God."

"When you go back, you will make mistakes. That is how you learn and grow. If you didn't make mistakes, you would be either perfect or dead. God created a world where you learn by your experience. The important thing you need to learn is to stop repeating the same mistakes over and over again. You have taken pleasure in defeating yourself. God wants you to grow spiritually by trial and error, but not to repeat endless cycles of self-defeating behavior. God wants you and every person to succeed in your spiritual growth. God wants you to become like the Christ, a son or daughter of God."

"But what if I make mistakes? Won't I be separating myself from God?"

"When you make a mistake, you need to consider what you did and why you did it. You should seek a better alternative. Tell God in the clearest way you know how what you did, why you did it, and what you are going to do about it. Before you can ask God's forgiveness you will receive God's forgiveness. God will erase your mistake from the collective memory of your life if, and only if, you are genuinely ready to be forgiven. You must regret your mistake and try to never repeat it again. God wants you to succeed."

"How can I be sure I am forgiven?"

"This is very important, that you understand God's forgiveness. When you ask God to forgive and you mean it from the heart, you are forgiven. To doubt or refuse God's forgiveness is an insult to God. Too often people ask forgiveness from God and refuse it. They live as if they are unforgiven. God wants you to be full of joy and grow into a wonderful child of God. God doesn't want us to carry guilt. God wants us to develop to our full potential as creative, joyful participants in the creation. When we ask God's forgiveness, it is given."

"If I go to heaven, I could become the person God wants me to become."

"You aren't ready to go to heaven. You haven't lived a life that is suitable for life in heaven. You have many things to learn in the world, and you still have your job to do, which is to take care of the people God needs you to love."

"Who am I supposed to love?"

"Your mother, father, sisters, brothers, wife, son, daughter, students, fellow teachers, and neighbors are your job to love. You were born to love those people."

"You can take care of them. You would do a much better job of loving them and helping them than I could do."

"We do love them and care for them, but you are the hands in the world to care for them. This is your job that you were created to do."

"The world will go on without me. I don't see why it is necessary for me to live in the world."

"You can save the world."

"I don't think so. I'm nobody and I'm not going to save the world. People who thought they were going to save the world are nuts. Most of them, like Hitler and Napoleon, were maniacs who did more harm than good. How could I save the world?"

"You are to love the person you are with."

"How will that save the world?"

"When you love a person, they will love the next person they meet, and they will love the next person they meet, and so on."

"What if one of those persons gets run over by a truck? Then it comes to an end."

"You are not alone in God's plan to save the world. There are millions of people loving people."

"There are millions of people hating one another, too."

"This is God's will, and it will be done. There are many more angels in the world than people trying to influence people to love and care for one another. All heaven prays for the world to change. It is God's will, and God's will be done on earth as it is in heaven."

"I don't know if I can do it."

"You can do it because we will help you."

"If you send me back, will it be like it was before? Will I be able to see you and hear you like I can now?"

"No, it will be like it was before, but we will be with you."

"I can't go back. I have never known love like the love you have shown me. I will die in the world from a broken heart."

"We will always be with you as we have always been with you."

"I know, but if I can't see you or hear you, it will be like you don't exist. I will die of a broken heart."

"There will be times when you will know we are close to you. You will feel our love."

"Can I ask you to appear to me?"

"No. If we appear, it will be very unusual. You can pray and you will know we are close because you will feel our love."

"How can I pray?"

"Call upon God. Tell God what you have done, both the good and bad things. Be completely honest with God. Don't hold anything back. God knows. You can't surprise God. God wants to hear it from you. Trust God. God loves you just for being you. Ask God for forgiveness for the things you have done wrong. Know God forgives you. Thank God for loving you and forgiving you. Ask God to fill you with God's love. Be very still and allow God to love you. You will feel the love around and inside you. You will know we are close."

"Do you promise that you will always be with me?"

"We promise."

"I think I could go back to the world if you are with me."

Then I was back.

❧

I was back in the bed that I had left earlier. The pain I suffered before this experience had returned with a vengeance, especially since I had come from ecstasy only to return suddenly to this agony. Beverly was sitting next to the bed, and I desperately wanted to tell her what had happened to me, but was unable to speak because I was gasping for air. Immediately, several nurses and orderlies came into the room and sent Beverly out, against her vehement protests. They had come to prepare me for the operation that I had long awaited. It was now around nine o'clock at night, and they announced that a doctor had arrived to do the surgery.

They lifted me off the bed and put me on a stainless steel gurney. Moving aggravated the excruciating pain I was already feeling, and I cried, asking them to be more careful. They removed my hospital gown and dry-shaved me from my chin down to my upper thighs. That was unpleasant enough, but what really hurt was their manhandling. They pulled on my limbs and stretched them out, they yanked on my privates in order to scrape them clean with the razor, and generally treated me with complete indifference. I couldn't help but compare them to the people that I had met in the place of darkness and wondered if they were somehow related.

As I was being pushed on the gurney down the hall, Beverly came alongside and grabbed my hand. I told her that everything was going to be fine. I was confident because I knew that I had God and the angels on my side, and that my life was not at an end just now because they had sent me back for a second chance. As soon as we arrived in the operating area, I was given an injection and lost consciousness.

11

WAKING UP

Bright white light shining in my eyes. Lying on my back staring into the lights, I noticed figures standing around me. They were pouring warm soapy water over my abdomen and gently scrubbing, then rinsing the suds away with cold water. As they repeated this several times, I wondered where I was. "Am I in heaven or is this earth?" I asked myself. Wide eyes looked closely at me from the masked faces. Then one of the shapeless figures rushed away and I heard them speak in French to one another. I began to realize that this was the world and they were doctors and nurses.

The nurse was telling a doctor that I was awake. He said that was impossible and came over to the table I was lying on. I closed my eyes because I felt uncomfortable seeing him when I was supposed to be unconscious. He berated the nurse for bothering him and went back to the other side of the room. The nurse bent over and looked into my closed eyes. I sensed her inches from my face, so I opened my eyes and smiled at her. I felt love for her, although I had never met her before. She was not amused. I wished I was in heaven and not back in the world. Then I fell asleep.

When I awoke next, I felt like my abdomen had been run over by a truck. There were a lot of tubes in me, and my whole body ached except my toes. I lay on a bed in semidarkness alone in a big room. There was a man on the other side of the room, bandaged from head to toe. How long had he been there? What had happened to him? Was he the reason they had waited eleven hours to do my surgery? Could he have been in a horrible traffic accident? Was he going to make it? I never found the answers to these questions.

Was my experience with Jesus and the angels real, or had I imagined it? Since it had happened just hours before, I began to compare it to what I was now experiencing. The sensations of sight, touch, taste, and hearing then were more vivid than my life experience of my senses. What was real? I knew that I would have to make changes in my life, but where to begin? In spite of the overall ache in my body, I was emotionally happy. I was basking in feelings of love and I wanted to share that love with somebody. Hours went by while I thought about all the things I had learned. Beverly came into the room. She looked so beautiful. She called my name.

I said, "I love you."

She said, "I love you."

"It's all love!"

"I love you."

"It's a huge ocean of love."

"Lots of people love you."

"I know, but it's all love."

"Yes, dear."

"You just let yourself go into the love."

She said, "How are you feeling?"

"I'm okay, but you have to let go and be in the love."

"Yes, dear, that's nice."

I knew that I wasn't getting through to her. I desperately wanted to tell her about everything, and she wasn't understanding anything I was saying. We talked a little while and she left. How was I going to tell her what I had experienced? How was I going to get her to let go and allow the love into her life? Would she believe me? Would anyone believe me? I must convince her. I didn't want her or anyone to go to the place of torment.

The next day was Monday and I was alone in the room except for the man covered in bandages. The room was dimly lit, when it suddenly became very bright. A young, attractive man was standing at the foot of my bed. He was about five foot ten with an athletic build and wearing a short-sleeve collarless shirt, white pants, and white shoes. He had short, light-colored hair. He knew my name and addressed me in English. I asked him his name, which was French, yet he spoke English with an American accent. He told me he had studied many years in the United States, then asked how I was doing. He was not deceived when I said I was fine. When he asked me again, I admitted that I wasn't doing well. He said he was watching over me and that he would continue to check on my condition. Then he added that I might not see him again, but that he would be near to ensure that my condition improved. We chatted a bit more and then he said good-bye. When he left, the room darkened to its normal state.

Right after his departure, a nurse entered the room and I asked her who the young doctor was who had just visited me. She said that her desk was just outside the door and that no one had been in recently. I described the man who had just left and she said it was impossible because she had been outside at the desk for a long time. I asked my wife and other nurses about him, and nobody knew anything about him. I then realized that he was an angel who had taken human form to comfort me and assure me that I was not alone.

Tuesday morning I was taken from the surgical recovery area back to the room I had been admitted to on Saturday. My roommate, Monsieur Fleurin, had been taken away for tests. Alone in the sunlit room, I began to despair that I would not recover from the calamity of the perforated stomach. I doubted whether anyone would ever believe my journey to hell and the meeting with Jesus and the angels. I wanted to tell my wife what had happened, but she seemed to doubt me. I said aloud in the empty room, "I'm not going to make it."

A voice said, "Get tickets to fly home Monday."

I looked around the room. It was empty. Who had spoken? I said aloud to the empty room, "How can I go home Monday when I am too weak to stand?"

The voice said, "You will be well enough to go home!"

I answered, "How can I believe you?"

It answered, "Believe."

A few hours later, my wife arrived for the two o'clock visiting time. I told her to buy plane tickets for Monday morning. We were going home.

Beverly said, "Okay, I'll be right back."

This was very strange because I was scheduled to be in this hospital for a month, and I was still too weak to get out of bed. I had fifty-six metal staples holding my abdomen together. My wife is a litigation attorney and doesn't do things impulsively.

But she went to the pay phone in the hall outside my room and called her parents in Iowa City, Iowa. She asked them if they could send two thousand dollars for plane tickets so we could come home. They called their banker, who told them that he would have two thousand dollars for Beverly to pick up in a half hour at a bank in Paris. Within moments, Beverly's parents called her back and told her where to pick up the money. Beverly came into the room and told me she was going to get the plane tickets and would be back in two hours.

A little after four, Beverly arrived with two tickets on TWA from Paris to Cincinnati, Ohio.

I said, "Why did you do that? It's crazy. How am I going to go home in a week?"

"Do you want me to return the tickets?"

"No."

"What do you want me to do?"

"I don't know."

"Why did you tell me to buy them if we can't use them?"

"I don't know. Why did you do what I told you to do?"

"I don't know."

Later, I asked her again why she had bought the tickets, because this behavior was so unlike her. She said she had been under a strange compulsion. We kept the tickets, hoping we would use them and not daring to get rid of them.

During the following days, I would talk to the unseen presence in the room that instructed me. I didn't know that this was prayer. The only time I heard that voice again was when I said it wasn't nice to tell us to buy plane tickets we wouldn't be able to use, and that we'd had to borrow the money from my wife's parents.

The voice said, "Believe!"

Wednesday, the intravenous tubes came out of my arms. The tube came out of my throat. One night I pulled the drain tubes out of my abdomen. On Friday they took out half the staples, and the remainder were removed on Saturday. I was running a high fever, but it didn't seem to concern the doctor or nurses. The eighteen-inch incision was healing well. Saturday my temperature was almost 40 degrees centigrade, which is 104 degrees Fahrenheit. The nurse said it was because I had left the thermometer in the sun, which I had not done. I hadn't been shaved or washed in a week and I was ripe. Beverly brought my clothes and shoes and toiletry articles. I was feeling so weak, a short walk exhausted me. I was certain I wasn't getting better. In fact, I knew I was getting sicker.

On Sunday morning I felt good, so I got up and gave myself a bath using the sink in the room. I washed my hair, my entire body, brushed my teeth, and shaved a week's growth. I put on the clothes Beverly had brought me and sat in the chair to wait for her.

When she arrived, I said, "I'm ready to go." We said goodbye to Monsieur Fleurin, who had been so kind. His parting words were, "It has been good to see your renaissance. Do you know the word, renaissance? Au revoir."

We walked to the nurse's station down the hall and announced that I was leaving the hospital. The nurse was astonished and ran to get a doctor. When he arrived, he said that I was not discharged. I informed him in my most authoritative manner that there must be a mistake because I was discharged and was leaving immediately. To our surprise, he agreed and went to fill out my discharge papers. In a few minutes we were on the street hailing a taxi to take us to the hotel.

That afternoon and evening in the hotel, I told my wife about everything that had happened in heaven and hell. Whether she accepted or not the fact of my experience I wasn't certain, but she was convinced that I believed what I was telling her. I talked for hours into the night, going over all the details of my experience when I was dying.

Early in the morning we went to Charles de Gaulle Airport and left for the United States. Beverly had wisely purchased business-class tickets. The seat fully reclined and I was spread out under five blankets. It was evident from the looks of the adjacent passengers that they were uncomfortable being next to a man who looked as sick as I was. When we arrived at JFK Airport in New York, Beverly got a wheelchair for me to make the journey to the next terminal. Our flight was delayed by four hours, and sitting in the wheelchair I began to feel very bad. Beverly said that we had better go to a hospital, but I refused.

I went into the restroom and splashed cold water on my face and prayed to God to give me the strength to get home. I came out of the restroom revived, and soon we boarded the flight to Cincinnati and home. I walked off the plane in Cincinnati and knew I was going to make it. We went home and I went to bed. Early the next morning we went to St. Luke's Hospital near our home, where our family doctor, Dr. Grover, was waiting for me.

He examined me and said, "I don't know how you made it here!"

"I have powerful friends," I said.

He admitted me to the hospital and I was put on the critical list. My diagnosis was double pneumonia, collapsed lung, extreme peritonitis, and non-A non-B hepatitis. I had a high fever, a distended abdomen, and was jaundiced. Many doctors examined me and began treating me with large doses of antibiotics and respiratory therapy.

My condition was worsening when Dr. Linne arrived after a few days. After an examination, all the bags of intravenous medicine were removed and new bags of antibiotics were hung. I asked the nurse what they were and she told me they were the most powerful new antibiotics available. I found out later that the massive doses of antibiotics I was being given could destroy the kidneys, but given my critical situation, Dr. Linne had made the decision that it was worth the risk. The surgeons had determined that I was too weak to undergo surgery to clean out the massive infection in my abdomen. My stomach swelled with infection. It looked like that of a woman seven months pregnant. The incision split open and foul liquids oozed out.

During those weeks I became increasingly weak and disoriented. Sleeping on and off day and night, I never knew what time of day it was or what day of the week. I couldn't watch television because it confused me. When people spoke to me, I had great difficulty comprehending what they said. I desperately wanted to tell people about God, Jesus, heaven, hell, and life after death. But whenever I tried to talk about these things, I became very emotional and my family insisted that I not talk about them. I was very frustrated since I both wanted to share and desperately needed to process all that had happened to me. I felt such strong love for everyone that I wanted to hug them and tell them that I loved them and that God loved them. When doctors and nurses came, I would tell them how much God loved them and that they were God's instruments for healing.

I found out later from some of the nurses that I was the joke of the hospital because of my ramblings. Here was this critically ill, jaundiced man professing love to anybody who entered the room and constantly babbling about angels, heaven, and God.

Many times during these five weeks at St. Luke's Hospital, I felt like I was going to die. The doctors always told me I was fine, but privately they told my wife that they didn't know whether I would make it to the next day. At one point I called my fifteen-year-old son and told him not to visit me. I didn't want him to see me die and I thought I was going to die that day. I was always confused and often agitated with visitors. I was losing my eyesight, too. I couldn't read or see clearly, and I could hardly understand what anyone said to me. I knew that I was becoming disconnected from the world. Inside, I was going over my Near-Death Experience every waking moment. I wanted to talk about it, but nobody would listen.

Several times during this period, when I was awake, believing that I would die soon, an angel came into the room. The room would fill with radiant white light, and the most beautiful figure of a luminous angel would appear by my bed. This happened only when I was awake, and I was amazed by the angel's appearance. The angel would assure me that I was going to live and that God was watching over me. I would immediately feel better physically and emotionally. The angel never came when someone else was in the room and always left before someone arrived. A nurse would often come into the room immediately after an angel had departed. I would be sitting up in bed, tears running down my face, and I would tell her that an angel had just been in the room. The nurses would always laugh and tell me to get some rest; I knew they didn't believe me. I also knew that the only reason I was alive was because the angels were helping me heal.

When the doctors said I was getting better, I told them it was because God was helping me. They were noncommittal in response. I wanted them to pray with me, but they were too busy. Dr. Linne was the only doctor who would listen to me talk about God's love.

The doctors began to tell me that it was a miracle I was alive.

I told them it was truly a miracle because God did it. I knew that the antibiotics and care that I was receiving were part of God's healing love. As God had inspired men and women to scientifically understand the mechanics of the human body and disease, God had given people the compassion to be instruments of God's healing power. Whether they knew it or not, the doctors and nurses were Christ's hands restoring health to the sick and life to the dying.

❧

Frequently I was offered pain medication, but I always refused it because I was already confused and didn't want to become more detached from reality. I was haunted by the anxiety of becoming increasingly detached from the world, and I did not know whether I would ever get back to normal.

The visitation of the angels was becoming a regular event, and when they weren't in the room, I was praying to God.

When people would come into the room, I was highly sensitized to their feelings. There were a number of occasions when I could see supernatural beings floating around them and sometimes through them. These beings ranged from light to dark, and from malevolent to benevolent. I had no idea what to do with these things I was seeing. On a few occasions I tried to ask the people in the room about their lives and whether they were feeling oppressed. It became clear to me that my inquiries made these people very uncomfortable. Apparently I had acquired the ability to see a dimension of reality that is not normally seen. But because I was so ill and vulnerable, I wasn't in a position to minister to other people.

No chaplain or psychiatrist ever came to see me. Many times I thought about requesting a visit but was afraid to because I did not know if anyone could handle what I wanted to tell them. I had become acutely aware of people's reactions to the little bit that I did tell them, and of their total disbelief. I was too weak and vulnerable to argue and defend my sanity. It was only after several months, when I had regained my strength, that I had the courage—and stamina—to begin to tell people about what had happened to me.

Over the years many people have shared their Near-Death Experiences with me, many of which were negative experiences. Most of these people have told me that they have not really shared their experiences with anyone because of the shame and ridicule they felt when they did attempt to tell about them. Based on the number of people who have told me about their negative experiences, it appears that these are not uncommon, and it is highly unlikely that anyone will ever hear about them. Since people who have had Near-Death Experiences need to process this information, and the best way for them to process it is by telling it to a nonjudgmental listener, there is a need for people in the helping professions, such as clergy, psychologists, doctors, and psychiatrists, to encourage people to share their stories without being judged or ridiculed.

12

LISA AND CLARENCE

During those five weeks at St. Luke's Hospital, I was on the critical list most of the time. I wanted to go home, to my *true home* with God and the saints in heaven. I had been told that I had a job to do in this world, but living in this world was too hard. I was losing my ability to see, to hear, to walk, and to communicate. What good would I be in this world? I was in constant pain. When I complained about the pain, they gave me medication that made it impossible to think. Thinking was the only faculty that I had left; losing that was worse than suffering the pain.

When the pain became so bad that I couldn't bear it, I would pray to God to give me relief. The more I practiced praying for relief from pain, the faster it would go away. The method of prayer I developed began with an address to God.

"God, you are everything and all that is. You are goodness, truth, light, and love. You know all and you love me. I am nothing except that you made me and love me. You saved me from death and the place of torment. You came to me and healed me. I know you as you were when you lived in this world and you know all about suffering because you have suffered. Have pity on me because I am weak.

"I want to be the person you created me to be, but I don't know how to do it. Only you can show me. I am caught up in my pain and it screams at me. It tells me I belong to it. It tells me I am nothing. It tries to convince me that you don't love me or care about me. Pain kills my hope and drowns my joy. It is stealing my life away from you. This suffering has no purpose except to seek your love. In the name of Jesus, I beg you to take this pain from me and give me peace. I will tell of your goodness even though they laugh at me. It doesn't matter because you are God.

"I thank you and love you because you hear my prayers, and you know the secrets of my heart even more than I know my heart. You can do anything and you want me to be alive and filled with joy.

"Thank you for loving me. Thank you for being who you are. Thank you for Jesus. Thank you for Jesus my friend."

After praying like this, I could feel the pain slowly decrease until it was gone. It always worked, sometimes more quickly than other times. Often the intense pain would interrupt my prayer and it would be difficult to focus on God. But I knew he could and would help me defeat the pain if I could persevere and focus my mind on him.

I continued to refuse all pain medication, and whenever pain overtook me, I would pray fervently until it was gone. Some days I spent most of my time doing that. When the pain came back, I would ask God's help and it would go away. I learned that I was completely dependent on God for every moment of my life. Every breath, every thought, every sensation was a gift from God.

I would tell anyone who would listen, "God is so good. God loves us very much. Just ask Jesus and he will come to you."

Everyone seemed to find this comical—except for Lisa.

Lisa was a recently graduated nurse in her early twenties. She worked the 11:00 P.M. to 7:00 A.M. shift. She would come into my room in the middle of the night, and I would be awake and tell her how good God is. She knew God, and she encouraged me.

Since entering St. Luke's Hospital, I hadn't been able to eat. I was on a liquid diet, which consisted of broth, tea, and Jell-O. Whenever I tried to eat or even sip a drop of water I became violently nauseous. I was being given fluid intravenously, but I was losing weight. I had gone from 235 pounds to 168. For the first time in my adult life, I could count my ribs.

I tried to eat but couldn't, despite the valiant attempts of my caretakers to get me to. One night Lisa asked me if I liked milk shakes. I told her I used to drink them all the time, but the thought of a milk shake made me sick. She said that she was going to make me a milk shake with real ice cream and protein supplement and I was going to drink it. I told her it would make me throw up.

She said, "You will drink it because I am going to make it with love."

I told her she was wasting her time.

Ten minutes later she returned with a huge chocolate milk shake. I told her I couldn't drink it.

She said, "I made this with love for you. Now start drinking."

How could I refuse? I started sipping on the straw. It tasted so good. Lisa stood over me while I slowly drank the whole milk shake. She just smiled and encouraged me. I didn't have any problems. The next morning I ate my liquid breakfast and asked for toast. From that day on, I began to eat and soon graduated to solid foods. As I ate, my strength came back.

Lisa had used the word that I couldn't refuse, love. She had the determination to make me eat because she believed in God's love. There is no doubt in my mind that she contributed to my healing as much as the doctors' medicine. She listened to me and understood how to communicate with me. And Lisa believed in the power of Love.

Across the hall from my room was a patient named Clarence, a man in his seventies who had severe Alzheimer's disease. He was kept in restraints because he was violent and unpredictable; he bit anyone who got too close.

Clarence was also a screamer. Especially during the night he would start howling like an animal. I never heard an intelligible word from him, just screams and howls. I began to hate him for making all his noise in the middle of the night. I hated him because he bit the nurses, the same nurses who were so kind to me.

I prayed that God would make him stop howling.

One night he was going at it and would not stop. I prayed and prayed that God would silence him and he kept on screaming. I asked God how such a thing could happen to a man that he would be reduced to such an animal state. God told me to listen to Clarence. I concentrated on his howling and then I understood what he was saying. He was screaming, "I'm alive! Don't you know I'm still me? I'm trapped inside, buried deep down in this body, but I'm still me. Can't somebody help me?" So I yelled back, "Clarence, I hear you! I know you're there! You're sick in the hospital. They are trying to help you. Let them help you. I know you're alive. I hear you!"

He quieted down.

Whenever he would start yelling, I would talk to him from

across the hall and he would quiet down. He just wanted somebody to know he was alive.

Clarence was locked inside a body and a mind that were failing rapidly. All that he ever was still lived inside of him; however, biochemical processes prevented him from expressing himself. What was expressed was frustration, anger, and sometimes resignation. From across the hall, I talked to Clarence and assured him that I knew he existed and I empathized with him. What a terrible existence, to be trapped inside a mechanism that doesn't respond and that is running out of control.

One night I had filled the urine bottle and had an urgent need to urinate. I pressed the call button for the nurse. After five minutes there was no response, so I pressed it again. Again there was no response. I kept hammering the call button, thinking that beating on it would convey my emergency.

Eventually Lisa came into the room. Agitated, I told her I had been calling for half an hour and had spilled urine all over the bed. She apologized for not responding and said that they'd had a "code blue" across the hall. I asked if the patient had lived, and she said no: they had worked on him for half an hour, but he didn't make it. I was ashamed of my anger.

Lisa stripped the bed and remade it with me in it. She bathed me and tucked me in to go to sleep. Would I ever be as good, as cheerful, as compassionate as Lisa? I thanked God for her and all the nurses, orderlies, housekeepers, and doctors whom God had given the heart of compassion to be his instruments of healing. Simple acts of kindness are as important to wellness as are the medical procedures.

13

SENT BACK

I was very weak for seven months following the surgery. When I eventually returned to work in January 1986, teaching my art classes exhausted me. During this time of recovery, I thought, studied, and prayed. My life had been lost and given back. Physically and spiritually I was born again. This rocked the foundations of all that I had previously believed, demanding that my entire life be rebuilt.

I had a myriad of critical questions that I needed to answer, such as: What had really happened to me? Why me? What was I going to do? How did I know it was not a dream or hallucination? Was it real?

All my life I had had dreams, but this experience was not a dream. When I had a nightmare, I would wake up. The experience in hell was far worse than any nightmare, but there I never woke up. My dreams had always had a sense of the surreal, but what I'd experienced after my "death" seemed more real than being awake. Rather than surreal, it was super-real. During that experience, my senses increased from above-normal to levels of sensation that are beyond explanation. I was more alive in every meaning of the word than I had been before or have been since the experience. There is no comparison between any dream state I know and my Near-Death Experience.

Could this have been a psychotic episode brought about by the extreme physical trauma of dying? I became obsessed with this question until it was resolved by several facts that collectively refute the explanation of trauma-induced hallucination.

Before the experience, anxiety and depression had spoiled my life. I justified my melancholia by convincing myself that this was the only state of mind a realist could have. I had believed there was no God, no heaven, no hell, no Christ, no angels, no miracles, no life after death, and no ultimate meaning to life. One is born into an utterly random universe; one struggles for survival and pleasure, then one dies. What was the point of living? There is none. Why not die? Too afraid to die, I kept on living.

Many times I had considered ending my life, but I always chickened out before I did it. Driving down the highway at ninety miles per hour late at night, thinking: just head into the bridge piers and it will all be over in a second, oblivion! I could never quite do it. Maybe one day I would have the courage.

There was very little joy in my life. In order to be happy I drank alcohol. At every social occasion, drinking was the means to a good time. The more you drink, the better you feel. The more you drink, the more you need to drink to get that high. Booze was happiness and lack of booze was melancholy. Alcohol use is encouraged in our society. In the circles that I ran in, one was expected to drink at social occasions. A party, going out for the evening, getting together at someone's home, going on vacation, visiting relatives, having dinner, sporting events, and other occasions were all accompanied by drinking. The only time one was supposed to not drink was at work.

After my experience, I quit drinking. The primary reason was I was happy and knew that alcohol would rob me of my happiness. Alcohol is a depressant that depressed people take to anesthetize themselves from their depression. I don't need it because I have a joy in my life that I want to keep. Alcohol degrades that sense of well-being with a counterfeit sense of well-being leading to depression in a vicious cycle.

My experience didn't frighten me out of drinking. It removed the need to drink. What kind of hallucination heals the soul?

After the experience, I wondered if I was the only person in the world who believed the understanding of God I had been given. As I read the Bible, I found everything that I had been told was consistent with the Bible, and most particularly with the Gospel stories about Jesus Christ. I would read a passage from the Bible and shout to my family, "This is exactly what they were teaching me!" I thought I had discovered the greatest book in the world. Every word spoke to me on a deep personal level. The Bible resonated with the truth as I had been given it. After weeks it dawned on me that I was not the first person to discover the Bible. Millions of people read the Bible and find the truth there. God speaks directly to us through the testimony of men and women as written thousands of years ago. The more I read the Bible, the more enthusiastic I became. Frequently when reading the Bible, the Spirit of God speaks directly to you. You shout inside, "Yes! Yes! Yes!" It is like discovering a magnificent jewel unexpectedly. I have found that the Bible speaks God's Spirit to us, but do we listen? Are we thirsting for the truth?

If my experience was a hallucination, and I shared the same beliefs with a billion living Christians and billions who had lived and believed before our time, then we all had the same hallucination. So be it.

I read other Christian writers like Thomas Merton and found kindred spirits. Merton's books were like milk to me. He could articulate our struggle with an understanding of God in a way that I could never hope to express. How strange that a Trappist monk knew and communicated to me on a deeply personal level. Our lives couldn't be more dissimilar, yet we were spiritual brothers. He was not psychotic. He was brilliant.

When I returned to teaching at the university, I was introduced to a professor in the Human Services Department, Dr. Scott Quimby. He had been studying Near-Death Experiences and we quickly became friends. Scott introduced me to literature on NDEs and took me to a meeting of the International Association for Near-Death Studies. There I found complete acceptance and interest in my own Near-Death Experience. Millions of people have had similar experiences, which validated my experience. Scott spent countless hours helping me process my experience. I thank God for sending him to help me grow spiritually and in understanding.

There is one overriding reason why I know my experience was not a product of my imagination. I should have died on June 1, 1985, but I didn't. Several doctors have told me that, under the circumstances, it is a miracle that I survived. I owe my life, my second chance, to God. When I called out to Jesus to please save me, I was dying. Jesus Christ came and rescued me and gave me life, faith, hope, joy, peace, and love. This happened in the midst of an extreme medical crisis. How can anyone explain that away? I certainly cannot pretend that I fabricated a new life during my misery. It's preposterous to suggest it. God intervened in my life, turned me around, and gave me a new spirit. God has done the same for millions of people.

One of the many benefits of my experience was that, before

reading the Bible or any other book on Christianity, I had been given a seminary education in Christian theology in talking with Jesus and the angels. I had never read anything on the subject, so it was surprising and delightful that I understood this complex topic before I picked up a book on the subject. Clergy whom I met after the experience remarked on my sound grasp of theology, and I knew I had been given this as a gift while I was dying in a French hospital. When I went to United Theological Seminary for three years of graduate study to obtain the Master of Divinity degree, my theology "lessons" served me well. What a joy it was to explore the earlier knowledge I had been given in greater depth with experts in the field. It was reassuring to find that what I had been taught during my Near-Death Experience was consistent with contemporary Christian theology. It was also helpful to know without struggling for the answers.

The gift of knowledge is only a part of the gift of faith. Faith means to trust God, and I have been given that assurance so fully, there is no reason to doubt God. Living life with faith is infinitely more rewarding than living without faith in God. Having faith gives one courage to do things one would never do, and the patience to endure the unendurable. Faith gives hope when you haven't a clue how things will turn out. Faith gives joy when everything is bleak. Life with faith in God is so superior to life without faith that I recommend anyone to seek faith above all other things.

Another reason I trusted the validity of my Near-Death Experience is the numerous encounters with supernatural beings in my years since. I have mentioned a few of these visitations in other chapters. Their timely help has kept me on the right path and safe from harm.

For example, a year after the experience, I was driving into the city on a bright, clear day. The exit ramp off the freeway made a long curving entrance directly into the center of downtown. The traffic light was green for my direction of traffic to proceed through the intersection. I was traveling at thirty miles an hour and there were no other cars in sight except one that had proceeded through the intersection before me. About twenty yards from the intersection I heard a loud voice say, "Stop! Danger!" Without thinking, I pressed the brakes hard and came to a complete stop just short of the intersection. As I was braking, a red pickup truck with dark-tinted windows came across the intersection against the red light at forty or fifty miles per hour. If I had not stopped, I would have been broadsided. Since there was no one around, my warning must have come from an angel. This kind of incident convinced me of angels' existence and the reality of my experience.

How God touches our lives is not something I question. I have been privileged to hear firsthand from hundreds of people about their extraordinary encounters with angels and Jesus Christ. These experiences are almost common but are too often kept private for fear of ridicule. The climate for religious experience is hostile in our society, and we repress the truth of God's intervention in people's lives.

After my experience, I wanted to talk with somebody about what had happened, but I didn't have any religious affiliation and didn't know any clergy. When I got home from the hospital, I called a nun who had been an art student of mine many years before. Sister Dolores was a history teacher at Notre Dame Academy, and we had kept in touch over the years. She was a fine person and we enjoyed talking about art. I asked her if she would come visit me. When she arrived, I was dressed in a bathrobe, wrapped in blankets, and sitting in a recliner. I said,

"Something very wonderful has happened to me. I have met Jesus." Then I began to cry, and I couldn't stop. The harder I tried to stop, the harder I cried. After half an hour, she said she had to leave. Patiently, she had sat opposite me and watched me cry. I begged her to come back and apologized for crying. She promised to return in a week.

When she came back, I managed to tell her my story in about an hour. She was silent through my telling. When I had finished, I asked, "Do you believe me?" She looked straight at me and answered, "Of course I believe you, but I wonder why it took so long."

"What do you mean, 'Why did it take so long?' "

"Do you remember the first time we met?"

"No."

"You called me over to walk with you after the first day of class. You said you were an atheist and didn't want any religion in the classroom."

"Oh, yes, I remember that."

"From that day, I have prayed for you every day, and I have had other sisters praying for you. That was thirteen years ago. I wonder why it took so long."

Sister Dolores had been praying for me to know God for thirteen years. When people ask me why I have been given this experience, I tell them Sister Dolores prayed for me for thirteen years.

There is another reason why I was given this experience of God. God loves a repentant sinner who wants to "come home." Jesus makes this abundantly clear in his story of the lost sheep and in the parable of the prodigal son. God waits for us and watches for us to come home. When we ask for God's forgiveness, we are forgiven.

Two factors kept me separated from God. The first was that I had deliberately separated myself from God and refused to acknowledge that. It wasn't God who had abandoned me, it was I who had left God. God had tried to reach me but I wasn't interested. Sin is intentional separation from God. We sin in many ways, and there can be no forgiveness until we confess our sins.

Second, I didn't believe in forgiveness. How easy it would have been to know God and receive God's love and forgiveness if I had known, but I didn't. God is eager to forgive when we are willing to acknowledge our sins and ask to be forgiven. I received a new life because I confessed and was forgiven. How simple it is and how much people resist doing it.

To be forgiven is to be given a second chance, to be given new life. We need only to make an honest confession and ask to be forgiven to have a new beginning. Love, hope, faith, and joy await us when we give it over to God.

14

NEXT TO HEAVEN

Although I felt an urgency to find a community of people who shared the same beliefs that I had so recently been given, I had no clear idea who or what that community might be.

In early August 1985, before I was able to drive again and when my ability to walk was still very limited, I asked my wife to take me to a bookstore. We went to the nearest mall and I shopped the religion section. I bought the *Bhagavad Gita, The Way of the Tao*, the *Buddhist Bible*, the Koran, and a concordance to the Bible. I had been reading the Bible exclusively and I had to be certain that I wasn't missing something. So I read the primary sources of other world religions. Even though I found inspired writing in all of these sources, they did not speak to me like the Bible did.

When I read the Bible slowly, prayerfully, openly, it was like having a conversation with God. It was, and still is, as if the words are alive. They resonate with vitality and excitement in my mind, as if I am engaged in a conversation with the divine. This was surprising, since I had tried to read the Bible on a few occasions in the past and had found it dry, lifeless, and confusing. The difference was in how I approached the Bible.

If you sincerely ask the Bible to speak to you, and read slowly, listening to every word, it speaks to your mind and becomes alive in your imagination. The more you allow it to speak, the more vivid it becomes. If you read it with indifference or cynicism, it doesn't respond. The Spirit of God that spoke to the hearts and minds of the writers of the books of the Bible will not impose its living word on an unwilling recipient. I had to ask the Holy Spirit to speak to me and reveal its truth to me. The spirit of truth wants to converse with us as long as we are receptive to know and grow in the divine conversation. Unlike any other written word that I have experienced, the Bible is alive with the Spirit of God.

My enthusiasm for discovering God's Spirit in the Bible was overwhelming. I would read verses to my wife and children, expecting them to have the same "Eureka" experience that I was having. Unfortunately, they did not share my enthusiasm, and I couldn't understand why. In the weeks after coming home from the hospital, I became a Bible-thumping zealot. The more my family resisted, the louder I shouted Bible verses. Mistakenly, I thought I could share the love of God by shouting scriptures. It was a disaster.

My recovery was progressing rapidly. In the evening, my wife would drive me to the university to practice walking. The first time I ventured about fifty feet and became exhausted, barely making it back to the car. Each evening we went to the same parking lot until I was able to walk the entire perimeter of the level lot. Then after days and weeks, I progressed to walking up and down hills and stairs. Every night was a small triumph of increasing strength and mobility. What exhilaration there was in climbing a stairway, walking normally instead of shuffling, and daring a few running steps!

Upon regaining my ability to walk short distances, I had the burning desire to attend a church. Which church, I had no idea. I prayed regularly that God would reveal to me the church I should attend. At times I would use the directory of churches in the newspaper or Yellow Pages to find the church, and nothing happened. After two weeks of praying and searching, I was so frustrated because I had received no answer, no sign, nothing. So I decided that I would select a church from the newspaper directory. I picked one based on the information that it met in a public school. This indicated to me that this church was not materialistic, since it didn't own property. God would surely be present in a nonmaterialistic church.

On Sunday morning, with much effort, I got cleaned up and dressed in suit and tie and off we went to a church fifteen miles away; a choice based solely on the fact that it didn't own property. When we got there we couldn't locate where the church met in the sprawling elementary school complex, and there wasn't a soul around to ask. Eventually we found a small note on a locked door that read: Closed for the summer. Reopening in September. Totally discouraged, we went home.

I blamed God for this failure. How could God let me go to a church that didn't exist? It had been a momentous decision for me to attend church for the first time in my adult life, and all I found was a locked door.

So I prayed and prayed. "God, show me a church to belong to. Where do you want me to go? I can't find one, but you know where it is. Give me a sign." After a couple of days, an artist friend, Beverly Erschell, called me to inquire about my health. During our conversation, I told her I was looking for a church.

She said that she went to a very nice church that was a mile from my house; the minister had a good heart and the people were a loving congregation. After the conversation, I asked my wife if she had heard of Christ Church. She knew it because she had attended choral concerts there, which our daughter had performed in. She said it was beautiful and close, and she seemed interested in trying it. So I prayed: Was this the sign I had been looking for?

Sunday morning came and again we prepared to go to church. This was a major undertaking for me because I was still recovering. My days were spent in a bathrobe, reading, praying, and sleeping. Getting up and out was a big event in my life, and I never knew when complete exhaustion would overtake me.

Off we drove to church. Then we couldn't find a parking space directly in front of the church, so my wife parked in the bank parking lot across the street. By the time we walked across the parking lot, across the street, and up the steps of the church, I was leaning heavily on her. What a pitiful sight I must have been to the greeters at the door of the church. Emaciated, jaundiced skin, yellow eyes, leaning on my wife, dragging my feet up the steps.

The worship had just begun with the congregation singing the opening hymn when we entered the sanctuary. A few feet inside, I saw on the ceiling of the church hundreds of angels basking in praise of God. They were a golden color and radiated golden light around them. The unexpected sight of the angels unleashed powerful emotions of awe of God from inside me. I did the only thing I could do in that circumstance, which was to throw myself down on the floor. Prostrate on the carpeted aisle, I thanked God and praised God profusely.

Regrettably, we were not in a Pentecostal church, where this might have been acceptable behavior. My wife bent over me, concerned that I had collapsed. The ushers rushed to her aid, asking if they should call an ambulance. Then my wife realized that I was in religious ecstasy and became furious with me because of the commotion I was creating in the back of the church. She was yelling in my ear, "Get up! Get up! We will never come to church again!" I was content to lie facedown on the floor and happily praise God. The ushers lifted me into the closest available pew, where I sat with my face in my hands weeping and thanking God and Jesus.

Beverly kept repeating that she was terribly embarrassed and we would never go to church again. I couldn't stop the tears of joy. Whenever the congregation stood up, said prayers, or sang, I just cried. Bent over in my pew, I was happier than I had been since the Near-Death Experience two months before. After we left church, there was a leaden silence on the ride home. At home Beverly said, "I have never been so embarrassed in my life. We will never go to church again." All week I begged her to give me another chance. I promised that I would not do it again. I would behave properly.

That week, the minister of Christ Church, Reverend William Crawford, came to visit me and asked about why I had come to church. I explained briefly what had happened in Paris and what I had seen in his church. He appeared nonplussed by my extraordinary story and invited me back. He said, "God has sent you to Christ Church and you belong there. God has sent me to you to help you understand your experience and to learn more about Jesus." That sealed our relationship then and there. Bill shepherded me like the good pastor he is.

The next Sunday we went back to Christ Church, and over the weeks I slowly resisted crying enough to sing the hymns and recite the prayers. I continued to see the angels and their beauti-

ful radiance in the upper portion of the worship space every
Sunday. I noticed that they were more splendid when the congregation sang and less radiant when things like announcements
and collections happened. I had the impression that I was the
only one who could see the angels. The prayers, hymns, scrip-
ture, and sermons all spoke to me in a deeply personal way because it was consistent with what I had experienced with Jesus
and the angels.

The people of the church were very kind and accepting without imposing themselves. I was amazed that we were welcomed
into the church without their knowing anything about us. They
just accepted us into their community without question. I discovered that these people were searching for God just as I was. I
admired them because they had been in God's house long before
me. I knew they were not so different from me, except they had
discovered the truth sooner.

The more I attended church, the happier I was. The minister
was surprised when I told him after a few Sundays that I wanted
to join the church. He offered me the chance to join a new members' class that he was just beginning. I learned that this church
was a denomination (United Church of Christ) that comprised in
part the Congregation Church I had been raised in. My sponsor
Beverly Erschell explained to me, "God wanted you to grow
where you were planted."

Had God planned all this before it happened? Twenty-three
years later, I had returned to the church I was raised in. In my
adult life I had done many things and lived all over the United
States, but had never gone to church once. Spiritually, I had wandered in the wilderness for over two decades and had now returned home.

Pastor Bill became my close friend, and he helped me grow

in many ways. I will be forever grateful for his patience and kindness to me in bringing me into his flock and nurturing my understanding of the Christian faith.

Christ Church United Church of Christ gave me more than I could ever repay. This community of faith is composed of ordinary middle-class people representing a wide spectrum of professions. I imagine that this church is typical of tens of thousands of churches in America. There is nothing exotic about it compared with other churches, but in comparison to the culture around it there is a vast difference. The main attraction of the church for me was the unqualified efforts to worship God and propagate the lifestyle of a follower of Jesus Christ.

When I returned to work at the university, I was in conflict between my Christian ideals and the worldly behavior of the people at the university. Many times I was horrified by the self-centeredness of the people I worked with in academia.

In the Christian Church the standard for what a human being should be is greater than any person has ever achieved. Jesus Christ gives a whole new meaning to what a human might be. In the secular world, achievement is valued and rewarded above all else. Moral behavior is determined by the lowest common denominator. The secular world seeks prohibitions against anti-social behavior, or what one can get away with. The church asserts a standard of behavior almost, but not quite, beyond human capacity. I found it increasingly difficult to live and work in both worlds simultaneously because of the difference.

Jesus Christ commanded his disciples to love one another as he loved us. I don't know how to practice this radical kind of love in a world that exploits love. One who takes Jesus Christ's command seriously must live in constant tension with the world. The fervent desire of the Spirit of God working in and through the church to make the world more loving is thwarted by the passion of the world to undermine the purpose of the church.

The Bible teaches—from the Book of Genesis to the Book of Revelation—that each of us is free to choose whether we are proponents of God's will or opponents of God's will. The question is: Are you seeking God's will or are you not? Knowing and doing God's will is the curriculum in this life. The church, as flawed as it may be, is the instrument to help us know God's will. The church is the closest we will get to God outside of heaven. The secular world is the place where we are sent to do the work of the Spirit of Christ.

15

LIMBO

After my Near-Death Experience in Paris, I was in limbo. I was obsessed with returning to heaven. The beauty, wonder, joy, and love of heaven were my heart's desire, and I had a case of terminal homesickness. I asked myself, "Why do I have to live in this world when I only want to go home?" It seemed impossible to be loving in a world that rarely even acknowledged God. What could the world have to offer that wasn't infinitely better in heaven? I felt stuck between heaven and hell. This world is neither heaven nor hell, but it is preparation for one or the other.

I was fascinated with the writer Thomas Merton and read every book of his I could find. My pastor, Reverend Bill Crawford, suggested we visit the Trappist abbey of Gethsemane, Kentucky, where Merton had lived as a monk. Secretly, I wondered if I would find what I was looking for in a life of prayer in a monastery. Perhaps God would give me a sign to become a monk. One bright fall day in 1985, Bill and I drove the three hours to the abbey.

When we got there, a monk welcomed us. We asked if he

would direct us to the grave of Thomas Merton. The monks live by a rule of silence except when conversation is necessary. Only the monks assigned to welcome guests have permission to speak. As we walked to the monastery's cemetery, the monk said, "There is something I want to tell you. This summer a brother in his late seventies woke up and was unable to move. When we discovered him in bed, it was evident that he was very ill. We wanted to take him to the hospital, but he refused, saying Jesus was coming for him and he was waiting in his bed for him. We then set up a prayer vigil around his bed. Every once in a while he would look up and say Jesus was getting closer. In the early afternoon he sat up in bed and announced, 'Jesus has come!' His eyes were wide open and he was smiling. He laid back in bed, closed his eyes, and was gone. I don't know why I told you this, but I felt compelled to tell you."

The monk then directed us to the grave of Thomas Merton, who was known as Father Louis in the monastery, and he left us alone. Bill sat on a bench while I prayed on my knees by the resting place of Father Louis. I was crying because I felt his presence near to me when suddenly a young man appeared by my side. He was wearing a sweatshirt and blue jeans. He handed me a book of Thomas Merton's poetry opened to a poem titled "The Cemetery at Gethsemane." After I read the poem, I understood that Thomas Merton had felt the presence of the saints buried there.

I gave the book back to the young man, closed my eyes, and said a brief prayer of thanks. When I opened my eyes the young man was gone. I was surprised because in the enclosed area of the cemetery there was nowhere for him to go. I looked around, but he had vanished. Confused, I went over to Bill, who sat facing toward me thirty feet away, and asked if he had seen the young man with the book. Bill said he had been watching me pray. He said, "The man appeared from nowhere, handed me the book, waited while I read the poem, took the book from me, and vanished." I asked him if he was certain. He assured me he was.

Later, when I was looking at photographs of Thomas Merton, I saw a picture of him when he was in his early twenties. He looked just like the young man in the cemetery!

I believe the spirit of Thomas Merton had visited me and consoled me at his grave. He reassured me that he understood my struggle of living in limbo between heaven and earth.

After a year of attending church, I had a growing compassion for the poor and hungry of the world. I wanted to do something more than put extra money in the collection plate on Sunday. After several weeks of praying about this, God answered my prayer.

During one Sunday morning worship service, the pastor invited a woman named Judy to speak to the congregation. She spoke for a few minutes about her experience at a soup kitchen being operated by a sister church as an inner-city mission. She invited anyone who was interested to speak to her after worship. When the service was over, we talked and made a date for the next Saturday to meet at the mission church at 8:30 A.M. There I met Reverend Jim Egbert, who had a ministry to the inner-city poor, which included the soup kitchen. Thereafter I worked every Saturday for four years at the soup kitchen. Reverend Jim continued to increase my responsibilities until I was begging for food, planning menus, recruiting volunteers, preparing food, serving, and cleaning up. This required about twelve hours a week. We served between 150 and 250 people every Saturday. I met many good people and became friends with volunteers and clients alike. I found it very rewarding to provide a wholesome meal for the needy. God was showing me that there was so much need for compassion in the world and not enough people willing to help. This world is not heaven, but it doesn't have to be hell. Every week there were miracles of donations of just enough food, money, and volunteers to provide a nutritious meal. Every week we started with almost nothing, and by Saturday morning we had just enough meat, vegetables, starches, and fruit for the people who came to eat. No one ever left hungry, and we seldom had anything left over. Early on Saturday mornings I had a couple of hundred pounds of food to wash, cut, cook, season, and serve, and there would be one or two people to help. It was impossible. Then a church group or family would show up and say they wanted to help. By the time noon came around, we were always ready for the line of hungry poor to feed. During this time I did a lot of praying and was never disappointed.

When you do God's work, God helps you do it. One time, I prayed that God would send us a big cash donation so we wouldn't have to manage the soup kitchen hand-to-mouth every week. A few weeks later a company gave us five thousand dollars. This money lasted over two years, buying supplies along with other donations. On Friday mornings, I would go to a large produce wholesaler and beg for produce. Every week they would fill the back of my truck with marginally salable produce. A farmer would arrive during the week and donate chickens to us. Bakeries gave us day-old bread. Someone would slip fifty dollars in my hand. God fed the poor through the hearts of people who gave time and gifts to care for the hungry. There is nothing we couldn't do if enough people listened to God.

During the same time that I served in the soup kitchen, I continued at the university as an art professor and soon became acting chairperson of the department as well. The previous chairperson's secretary had resigned, but a new secretary couldn't be hired for months. The timing couldn't have been worse for me; I had already arranged to take my family on a three-week trip to my ancestral homeland of Finland and wouldn't be able to participate in the hiring of my secretary. I was very anxious about this because that role is critical to the success of the department's operation. Yet I had no input in the hiring process. While I was away in Finland, I prayed that God would send me a secretary who was a Christian. I wanted someone I could pray with for the good of the department.

When I returned I met my new secretary: Janet Neltner. I didn't know how to approach the subject of her faith, so I asked her if she was interested in spiritual things. She said, "Yes." I didn't pursue the subject because she seemed uncomfortable about it. That night I was at my church and told a friend about my predicament with my new secretary and how I hoped she was a Christian. She asked the name of my secretary. When I told her the secretary was Janet Neltner, she said, "Janet Neltner is the most spirit-filled woman in northern Kentucky."

The next day when I went to work, I called Janet into my office. I said, "I am a Christian and I prayed to God to give me a Christian secretary. Why didn't you say anything to me?" She told me she had left her old job because they weren't Christians and she had prayed for a Christian boss! She didn't know if I was a Christian and was afraid to ask.

For the next three years we worked together, prayed together, and shared our faith, encouraging each other. Janet was a spiritual sister to me and I was her spiritual brother. I couldn't have done my job as administrator without Janet. I would not have grown in my faith without her influence. It is no coincidence that we were brought together. In fact, there is no such thing as coincidence. God works in mysterious and wonderful ways to make this world more like heaven. Janet helped me find God at work and in the world in general. We can find a little piece of heaven in the world. My homesickness diminished.

Helping so many students who were looking for answers to their spiritual questions became my secret career as an administrator. When I came back to the university after my illness, my superiors warned me that I should never discuss religion with students. In spite of this, an endless procession of students was waiting to talk to me about spiritual matters. My secretary, Janet, would pray for me when my door was closed, and she knew there was an attractive young female in my office. She was concerned they would seduce me, but she didn't need to worry because they were only looking for a friend, not a lover. Students in the arts are a most interesting, lively, and creative people. It was a privilege to know so many of them and to have them share their lives with me. I always tried to encourage them to live the faith they had been given and to trust in God. There is an enormous unmet need amongst college students for spiritual guidance. They are hungry for a relationship with God. Too often they choose not to turn to the church because the church is too tradition-bound and dominated by the interests of older generations.

My life as an artist was taking a surprising direction. When I completely changed my style of art in an attempt to represent spiritual concepts, I found there was little market or interest in art that explored these concerns. Galleries that had previously been exhibiting and selling my work told me they couldn't exhibit or sell my new work because no one was interested. I tried exhibiting in churches, but there was no interest in contemporary art that explored spirituality in unconventional art forms. It's ironic that the church was at one time the patron of artists and now has become indifferent to art. The art world is biased against religion. The creative spirit is one of the attributes of God that has been given to humans to express the divine in this world. The art world and religious establishments are indifferent or openly hostile to each other. Too often what is called spiritual in the art world is sophomoric hedonism at best and satanic seduction at its worst. Makers of the visual arts, music, the performing arts, and literature have the capacity to express our highest beliefs such as Michelangelo, da Vinci, Bach, Handel, Shakespeare, and Milton did. One gets a glimpse of heaven in the great art of the past. Today our culture encourages artistic expression that demeans the human spirit. I find no place for my art in this culture. Rather than trying to find an audience for it in an indifferent world, I create my artwork solely for my own gratification.

Creating art had been my driving passion in my life. Now I had to find a different outlet to express myself. I found this in working with people. Creating responses for people is more challenging than working with inanimate materials. Cultivating personal relationships has become my artistic expression.

In 1988, I was invited to spend three days at a Methodist church on an Emmaus Walk. This is an intense time of learning about the Christian faith and interacting with other seekers. In the Catholic tradition this is called Cursillo. We heard lectures, sang songs, shared deep feelings, and worshipped together. People's lives are changed and faith is found at greatly accelerated rates during these three-day events. I saw the Spirit of God work in dramatic ways in the lives of the forty or so men who were on the walk with me. This time of seeing the Spirit of Christ in my brothers further persuaded me that I needed to work full-time in faith-building.

I had been living in limbo for several years. The world was not my home, but God wasn't ready to take me to my heavenly home. When we know the love of God, we need to share that love. There is so much spiritual poverty in the world that I had to share the love I had been given. We can find a little bit of heaven in this world.

Eventually I left my position as a professor at the university to attend seminary full-time to train for full-time service in the church. God has kept me busy ever since. Sometimes I've been too busy, but the rewards are out of this world.

16

TELLING THE STORY

I t was about six months after the experience that I first told my story to a group of people. My friend Johnny had invited me to his Bible study group, led by a Catholic priest named Father John. About a dozen people were in the group, which had been meeting monthly for several years. When I told my story, I was astonished to find acceptance and understanding. The welcome was so strong that I joined the Bible study group for two years. I was completely surprised that normal people believed my fantastic conversion story and valued it. Little did I know then that I would tell the story hundreds of times to groups large and small.

I have met people and received letters and phone calls from people who heard my story and claimed that it was beneficial to them. If one person is helped to grow in an intimate loving relationship with God because of my testimony, then I believe it has been worthwhile. I believe God will bless someone by this written account.

God works in mysterious and wonderful ways to build our

faith. God has used my testimony in powerful ways. My hope is that I speak to the heart of the doubter and the unbeliever.

When I began telling my story, I didn't want to offend anyone. This caused me to be vague about certain things I had been told. After speaking to so many groups that have included mainline Christians, Hindus, Mormons, agnostics, Pentecostals, Jews, New Agers, cynics, doctors, scientists, and others, I realized that it is better just to tell it unvarnished and let them decide for themselves what relevance it has to their life. My responsibility is to be faithful to the truth as it has been revealed to me by God and according to my understanding.

Testimonies have a power to connect us with one another. Our stories that share our personal experience of the divine support us in our spiritual journey. The history of faith in God has been built on personal testimony. The Bible is a collection of testaments, and the New Testament Gospels are the most amazing testimonials to God's love for all people.

I pray that you will find my story to be consistent with the Gospels of Matthew, Mark, Luke, and John. In particular, I suggest that you look at the story of the Prodigal Son in the Gospel of Luke. This is my story.

Jesus told this story to teach anyone who wants to come home to God about the love of God. The father, who signifies God, runs to meet his returning prodigal son and welcomes him with a great celebration and gifts. With millions of others, I claim this story as my own. As I have grown in my spiritual journey, I have come to identify with the elder son and the father as well as the prodigal son.

Would you run down the road to welcome the repentant son who squandered half of your worldly goods? Would you resent a prodigal brother who returned while you had remained faithful and hardworking? The power of the story of the Prodigal Son is its insight into human nature and the awesome love of God. The Bible is full of stories like this. Stories of people with human frailties whom God loves and redeems. My life has followed the same pattern.

The power of God works through these stories to change our lives. It was the power of God that worked in the lives of a few men and women telling stories about Jesus Christ that conquered the mightiest empire in the history of the world. Rome was conquered by the Gospel stories, which have the power of God's Spirit in them.

Today we have a new empire to conquer. It is an empire of pride. Too many people are separated from God, one another, and themselves. Lies masquerade as truth, and exploitation is disguised as enlightenment. There may never be total agreement on the details of the solution to our problems, but we need to achieve consensus on the essentials. The fundamental understanding of God and humanity needs to be achieved before we will be able to devise solutions to the problems facing us.

Telling my story is part of a global spiritual revolution. My part is no more important than your part in the beginning of God's reign in the hearts of humankind. The leader of this movement is the Holy Spirit. I was told during my Near-Death Experience that this is the time for people to decide and to act. God did something to change the course of human events two thousand years ago and has been patiently waiting ever since. This is the day the Lord has made for us to become the sons and daughters of God.

The signs of the times are everywhere around us. Even the popular culture of television is showing increasing awareness of God. When commercial television produces top-rated programs featuring angels and clergy in positive situations, it is the Holy Spirit and the public driving this programming. The enthusiasm for direct experience of God's Spirit is changing the style of worship across America and the world. Traditions of passive participation in worship are dying, and people are flocking to churches that offer active participation in worship. The distinction between formally trained clergy and the ministry of all people is blurring. The authority of the formal church is becoming increasingly irrelevant in the increasing authority of the Holy Spirit directly experienced in people's lives. God is breaking into people's lives in unprecedented ways.

Experiences of God are the source of many popular books. It is becoming common for famous athletes, actors, politicians, and other celebrities to speak about God and their religious convictions. This is the beginning of a tidal wave of transformation that will sweep across the earth.

Many religious leaders are expressing tolerance and respect for differing religions. God creates variety in everything he does, and we will ultimately find the same God, the same Christ, the same truth in all religions. The differences between religious beliefs are man-made. The essential truths underlying religions are God-inspired. The Spirit of God will bring us to the truth.

Near-Death Experiences are one small component in the great transformation taking place in the world today. People are telling their stories of their experiences of God. The conversion of the world to faith, love, and peace is happening. It happens one person at a time. You can find it in the marketplace, the workplace, the home, and in churches and temples. This is what the heavenly teachers told me would happen.

In the telling of my story, I have been telling you an old, old story, one that goes back before history. This story makes visible the invisible in our lives. What we have been blind to, now we see. When you get it, you will never let go. The message has never changed. The message is how much God loves us and cares about us. The message is how we can respond to this great love.

I give you my story in the hope that you will find or more fully appreciate where God is in your story. You and I are very special in God's eyes. God wants us to live in joy, peace, hope, and love. God wants us to come home.

17

A SECOND CHANCE AT LIFE

One of the questions I'm most often asked when I talk about my conversion experience is, "Why did God give you this second chance?" There are several reasons why I believe God gave me this second chance at life.

I should have died in Paris on June 1, 1985, because of the ten-hour delay before undergoing surgery for the perforation in my stomach. The doctors in the United States said that I should have lived for five hours. Yet no one examined me during the nine hours I waited in the Paris hospital for the operation. It is impossible to claim that I died, since I received no medical attention during that time.

Ten days after the operation, I entered St. Luke's Hospital in Kentucky. There I was placed on the critical list, where I remained for four weeks. The doctors told me it was a miracle that I survived the complex of critical diseases I had.

Whether I died during my Near-Death Experience depends upon your definition of death. There is no question that I was dying.

I do know that in a moment I went from death to life. My entire life was radically changed when by all accounts I should have been dead. The only reason I am alive today is because God intervened and gave me new life physically and spiritually.

God intervenes directly in the lives of many people. A Near-Death Experience is only one of the many ways that people's lives have been radically altered. According to surveys, as many as one in twenty people have had a Near-Death Experience. However, countless people have had profound life-changing experiences in other ways. Life-changing experiences have occurred during contemplation, recovery from addiction, during worship, in extreme emergencies, and under the duress of combat. Hundreds of people have told me about the mystical life-changing experiences they have had. The ultimate significance of these events depends, however, on what people do with them afterward. When God touches someone, where does that person go from there? We are always free to choose how we will use our lives and what changes we are willing to make.

God gave me a second chance because Sister Dolores had been praying for me for thirteen years. She also had other sisters praying for me. Johnny and Shirley, my former neighbors, were praying for me. One of the most powerful things we can do is pray. Prayer can change the world.

When I was dying, I was taken to the entrance of hell. The depth and vastness of hell is far beyond what I experienced. Some would call what I saw purgatory. During that time I called out to Jesus to save me. The sacred scriptures of the Bible say in several places: "Anyone who calls upon the name of the Lord shall be saved." I called on Jesus to save me, and he did.

The memory of trusting in Jesus came to me from a distant time when a Sunday school teacher had taught me about Jesus and his love. In the innocence of childhood, I was able to call upon him. When I was twelve, I asked to be baptized. The Holy Spirit was working in my life. In my late teens I rejected the faith I had been given. Even though I had denied my faith, the Spirit of Christ was always inside me.

Looking back over my life, I see many situations where there was a spiritual battle going on inside me. My ego had developed as a rugged individualist, but inside was a pursuit of God. This battle had been going on for years and intensifying until it erupted in a spiritual emergency.

I blew a hole in the center of my abdomen because of this spiritual conflict. This physical trauma was directly related to the spiritual struggle I had been fighting. There is no point in wondering what would have happened if I had done this or that differently. What happened was the inevitable consequence of my actions. I am responsible for what happened.

Most important, the reason God gave me a second chance was because God loves me. God gives all of us second, third, fourth, fifth, sixth, seventh, and more chances. This was not my second chance. It was one in a long series of second chances I had been given. I had taken God's love for granted too often.

After my conversion, I expected to be perfect in every way. This never happened. I was horrified when I became angry over little things. I thought I would do better than that. My soul's journey is similar to that of everyone else I meet. I find myself doing those things that I do not want to do, and not doing those things that I want to do. Even though I sometimes feel like a wretch, it is the Spirit of Christ inside of me working and making me complete. As long as I am in this world living the human life, I will have the struggle of being a child of God and being a child of this world. The love that I give will cover the multitude of mistakes that I make. My trust is in the power of Jesus Christ to raise me up when I die.

In retrospect, I am making progress in my spiritual development over the long range. Looking back over the short term, I fall back and move forward, veer right and then left. The climb is not straight up, but there is progress. God doesn't expect anyone (including me) to become instantly perfected. God only asks us to try. God loves us exactly as we are and desires that we grow spiritually in love. When we love God, love our brothers and sisters, and love ourselves, our Maker is pleased.

The best way to grow spiritually is in service to others. We will find purpose and development in relationships to other people. We imagine that we are isolated from others, but the opposite is true. How we interact with others is our soul journey. What we think we are is not who we are. How we live lovingly with our brothers and sisters is who we truly are. If you want to grow spiritually, examine how you are expressing love, joy, peace, kindness, generosity, patience, and faithfulness toward others.

Jesus and the angels told me, "God wants us to care for one another." Love the people you are with by being totally present to them. We are responsible to God for changing the world by changing ourselves. How you give your attention to the person you are with is the way you change the world. The greatest commandment is to love one another.

Prior to June 1, 1985, I lived my life in the pursuit of happiness. There were fleeting moments of sensual or ego gratification. Generally I wasn't happy; in fact, I was mildly depressed much of the time. Happiness comes and goes. God wants us to have joy in our hearts. This joy that God gives is distinctly different from happiness, which is transitory.

Ever since June 1, 1985, I have had joy in my heart. I have had moments of the full range of emotions, but the joy stays constant. Real joy is independent of the events in our life. Joy is being in an intimate relationship with God. Joy knows the love of God. Joy is trust that all things work for God's good purpose for those who love God. Joy knows that every emotion, including fear and suffering, can bring us closer to God. Joy is allowing God to be our God. Joy knows the Spirit of Christ in every moment of our life.

Joy is recognizing the Spirit of Christ in every person you meet. No matter what people appear to be, they are children of God, and the Spirit of God is in them (somewhere). We can love the Spirit in them even when we resist the evil they do.

Yes, we are all flawed individuals. None of us is perfect. Once, while on a retreat a year after my transformation, I was talking to a Mennonite woman. During the conversation I said I was no saint. She became very grave and said, "You are a saint."

I responded, "I certainly am not."

She answered, "Are you beloved by God?"

"Yes," I said.

"A saint is anyone beloved by God and who knows it."

We are saints (in process) because of God's holy love for us. We become saintly when we understand this and live accordingly. We have been chosen by God to be a holy people. This begins when you know how great God's love is for us. My experience was about discovering how God loved me. I beg you to examine the love God has for you. God invites you and me to be saints together.

18

ANGELS

During my Near-Death Experience, I was given wonderful insights into the beings we call angels. Angels are messengers of God. There are uncountable kinds of angels. Their number exceeds the stars. In the most general sense of the meaning of the word angel, we are to be angels to one another.

God speaks to us through the creation, through sacred literature, through our experience, in our capacity to reason, through creativity, and through people. God most often speaks to me through people. The issue is not whether God speaks to us. The issue is whether we listen. It was shown to me in my experience that God had spoken to me frequently during the decades of my life when I doubted God's existence. One of the ways God spoke was through people.

An art student named Michael Smith was an outgoing and flamboyant character. He was also a homosexual and a drug user. After he graduated from the university, I lost contact with him until one day I was informed that he was dying in a nearby hospital. I went to visit him to say good-bye. What a shock to see his emaciated body in the hospital bed. It was even more surprising when he talked to me and shared his joy about his newfound faith. Michael told me that when I knew him, he was promiscuous, used drugs heavily, and was involved with satanic rituals. When it was discovered that he was terminally ill, he began to think about his life and regretted many of the things that he had done. He looked me in the eye and was radiant with joy, saying, "I prayed to Jesus Christ and he came to me and forgave me. I am not afraid to die because I belong to him and he will take me to heaven."

I didn't know what to say, but I was astounded that this man was so confident and joyful despite the fact that he was so near to death. He was God's messenger to me even if I wasn't listening. In some way he had planted a seed in my mind that bore fruit when I was close to death.

The love of God that Michael shared with me as he was dying was profound. I was not receptive to what he had to say, but I couldn't deny that he had found peace of mind, joy, hope, and love in the worst of circumstances. Michael died two days after I visited him, and I couldn't help but wonder if his deathbed confession was relevant to me. But I refused to listen.

The angels showed me many instances where they had tried to speak to me about God, but I had shut them out. They spoke through people who were inspired by God.

It was easy to ignore and ridicule the Bible-thumping evangelists who appeared on the university campus to harangue the students. It was not so easy to dismiss the witness of people whom I knew and admired. Joanne was an art student who often spoke to me of her love of God. I just smiled and tried to ignore her. She didn't preach at me, she just testified her love of God and Christ.

No person can give you faith when you are unwilling to receive it. Faith is the basis for loving God and knowing God. The angels' primary desire is to give us faith in God so we will receive God's love and know God in an intimate way. The angels will never force us to have faith. They offer it to us continually, no matter how many times we reject them. The angels had spoken to me through a dying man, a beautiful young lady, and countless other people. The angels never give up on us.

Angels sometimes appear to us as people. Angels can take on any appearance they wish. We have encountered angels and did not realize they were angels in human form.

After my conversion, I went on a series of retreats encouraged by my pastor to help me understand where my spiritual journey was taking me.

During an eight-day silent retreat at the Jesuit Renewal Center in Milford, Ohio, I was struggling with how I could share God's love with people. I had learned that people hate being preached at. As a college professor, I had given information to students by lecturing. This worked relatively well with a group of people who were paying for information. How do you communicate faith to people who are indifferent or hostile to the message? I desperately wanted to share the love of God, but had met constant rejection outside the church. I implored God, "Why have you given me this desire to share your love with a world that doesn't want it?" After six days of silent contemplation on this question, I was no closer to an answer than when I had started.

On the seventh day of my retreat, I wandered into the chapel of a large nursing home near the retreat center. This facility had formerly been a Jesuit seminary, so the chapel was large and beautifully adorned.

I sat in a pew and prayed that God would answer my question of how to share God's love. After a long period of silence, I heard a faint voice say, "H eight." What could this mean? I listened intently and heard "B two." What was God saying? Then I heard "N fourteen." I stood up and went to the open window and realized that I was hearing the caller of a bingo game drifting into the chapel. I laughed at my stupidity. Then I said aloud, "Thanks a lot, God. I came here with a serious question and you play jokes on me."

As I walked out of the chapel, I noticed a pamphlet on a table by the door. I picked it up and opened it to the middle. The only thing printed on the page was, "You will see the love of God in the smile of a child. Mother Teresa." I put it down and walked out of the nursing home.

On the steps, coming directly toward me, was a girl about nine years old. She was dressed simply and looked beautiful. She approached me, standing directly in front of me. Then she smiled. I stood frozen. Her smile was filled with love and acceptance. I felt such strong love from this complete stranger, I didn't know what to do. She walked around me up the steps. I turned to speak to her and she was gone. I followed after her, but she had disappeared. I began to cry. God had answered my prayer. An angel had shown me love and acceptance. That is how we are to share God's love with one another. The stranger you meet could be an angel.

Angels rarely appear in their glory. The times that angels have appeared to me in their full glory, it was almost unbearable. The brightness of the light that radiates from them is brighter than the light from a welding torch. Their light doesn't burn the eyes, but it is frightening because it is so different from our experience of life. An experience of the supernatural glory and power of an angel is frightening. They don't appear to us in their natural state very often. They most often tone it down for us to keep us comfortable. I don't have the words to adequately describe angels in their natural state. Brighter than lightning, beautiful beyond comparison, powerful, loving, and gentle are words that fail to describe them. Artists' depictions of angels are pitifully inadequate. As an artist I am aware of the impossibility of representing an angel. How do you paint something that is more radiant than substance? How do you paint colors that you have never seen before or since? How do you describe love on a canvas?

Angels are with us constantly and they are everywhere. We are never apart from them. We have angels who guard us from evil. Thousands of stories have been published concerning angels intervening in people's lives. Why they intervene sometimes and other times don't is between them and God. They told me that they always want to intervene in our lives, but sometimes God restrains them. God wants us to experience the consequences of our actions. On special rare occasions God allows the angels to help. When we ask God for spiritual gifts of love, faith, and hope, God always allows the angels to help us. Spiritual gifts are never refused if we are ready to receive them. The angels are working all the time to give us the love of God, faith in God, hope in God. Angels hear our prayers.

Angels do not want to be worshipped. They want all praise to be for God. They don't want us to confuse them with God. They know the difference between the Creator and the creature. They are servants of God, created to be God's messengers. We can thank them for being that for us.

Angels don't make mistakes, because they communicate directly with God. Their will and desire are the same as God's. We can ask God to send angels to guide us and protect us. We can ask the angels to teach us God's will. We can't make the angels appear to us or do anything that is not God's will.

There are different kinds of angels with different responsibilities and different attributes. One angel may accompany a child, another has the responsibility for a city, another a nation, another a world, another a universe. We might think that the mighty angels are gods, but they don't think of themselves that way. They know they are servants of God participating in the divine plan. Angels love God with their whole being. They desire nothing but to serve God. Angels can experience what we think and feel. When this is consistent with God's will, they are joyful. When we are opposed to God's will, they suffer emotionally. If we knew how empathetic our angels are with us, we would want to please them and God. We would never want to do anything that would distress them, but we do. The Spirit of God is the spirit of the angels. This same Spirit is in us, leading us to truth and love. When we allow the Holy Spirit to guide us, we are in harmony with the angels and God. Then we become like the angels, messengers of God.

The best word to describe an angel is compassion. As we live by the Holy Spirit, our compassion grows. The compassion of the angels for us becomes our compassion for all people. We discover that the love of God is tough love. The love we learn is complex and difficult. Just as the angels refuse to control us, we understand that we shouldn't control one another. We can try to influence, but we can't control spiritual development. Worldly things we have power over, and we are to use this power for good. Spiritual things we can only influence.

Angels can move through time and space as easily as thinking. The laws of physical nature do not bind angels. Angels are aware of and protect us from forces we don't know or aren't capable of imagining. Our angels are ever-vigilant to protect us from evil that originates from other dimensions of the unknown universes. We don't have to worry about it. We should just be glad they are there keeping us safe. There exist supernatural beings that seek chaos. They have no power over us except the power we give them. They are known as demons, the devil, or evil spirits. They should be rejected as much as possible. The power of God and the power of God's angels is much greater than theirs. The best defense against evil is to be filled with the Holy Spirit.

The martyrs could suffer excruciating torture because the angels revealed themselves to them. Heaven was opened to them and torment became bliss. In times of danger, pray to God to open heaven to you. Invite the angels to show themselves to you. Ask Jesus to save you. This world will fade away.

The angels are so complex in number and type that we could never understand fully, even with a complex "angelology." Angels are God's compassion. That is more than sufficient. They minister to us for God. Thank God for your angels.

19

PILGRIM

During my Near-Death Experience, the most important lessons I was given by Jesus and the angels were:

1. God is with us. The Spirit of God wants to be present in everything that we do. Enlightenment is to see God working in every moment. The reality of the Spirit of God is the way of life.

2. God loves you more than you can possibly comprehend. God has given you this life so you can grow spiritually. The gifts you have been given are the attributes of God. We have been made in the image and likeness of God. These gifts are emotions, consciousness, free will, reason, love, soul mates, the physical universe, and the Holy Spirit. We can perceive God in us and through us in each of these divine attributes.

3. In my Near-Death Experience, I was told that God has emotions. Our emotions are like God's emotions. Our emotions can either direct us toward the will of God or away from the will of God. Emotions are the engine that drives us. Emotions are the force that desires to make us Christlike or

turn us into the adversary of God. We are not controlled by our emotions. Feelings of happiness, pleasure, pain, anxiety, anger, and despair can lead us to a greater appreciation of God and a life of thanksgiving. All emotions are part of our thinking process. How we use our emotions is our choice.

4. Heaven wants us to give our feelings to God. Allow the Spirit of God to show you where these emotions come from and how you can direct their powerful energy to align your life with God's plan. If you are feeling pleasure or depression, let God's Spirit give you insight into where these feelings are coming from. How can you use this energy to drive your purpose in accordance with God's purpose for you?

   Anger about injustice can motivate you to resist evil and conquer evil. Feelings of sexual desire bond man and woman into an intimacy that can lead to lifelong partnerships in marriage. Sexual desire expressed wantonly leads to dissipation of intimacy and trust between partners. Jesus expressed God to us when he had compassion for the woman caught in adultery, when he used anger to cleanse the temple, when he felt pleasure eating with outcasts of society, when he wept at the death of Lazarus, and when he felt the power to perform miracles. During my time in eternity with Jesus, I felt his complete empathy with me.

5. We must become conscious of ourselves. I was told that it is imperative that we bring rigorous self-examination before God. Through our confession we are healed and forgiven.

6. Find your soul mates. God brought my wife and me together to learn love. I saw it in my life review. God gives us one another to learn how to love. Jesus told me, "This is your job." Other pilgrims expand our awareness. It is through our soul mates that God most often speaks to us. Seek people whose

spiritual journey is similar to your journey. Demand truth in love from your soul mates. Jesus said, "Where two or more are gathered in my name, there I shall also be."

7. Free will is the ability to make choices. God has given us this greatest of gifts. This freedom to do what we will is an amazing gift of love that is taken for granted. Even though we may imperfectly know God's will in the choices we make, our intention to choose God's perfect will please God. We were put in this world to know and to do God's will. That is the whole life experience.

8. God has given us the power of reason to create ourselves in the image and likeness of God. Reason enables us to make the best choice. The dilemmas we face in life are manageable through the use of reason. God doesn't demand our blind submission, rather God invites us to the truth through reason.

9. God gives love. God's love is unconditional. God gives love freely. God's love seeks only to be expressed. When you become aware of God's love, you only want to share that love with others. We need to put our love of God into action instead of theory. Love puts the needs of others ahead of our own needs. Jesus' love for us is the extreme love of God for us.

10. The physical world of matter and energy is the beautiful creation God has given us for our enjoyment, care, and edification. We have abused our responsibilities to the planet, and it is time to rethink our relationship to the resources, plants, and animals that God created out of love. If we imagine God as the ultimate artist and we inhabit this masterpiece called Earth, how have we carelessly exploited our dominant position? All the science and technology that we possess was inspired by God. We must seek a more harmonious relation-

ship with the natural world. This is a holy place and we should walk with reverence upon the earth, as Jesus did.

11. God's Spirit will make us whole. The Holy Spirit is God's presence in our lives. The Holy Spirit leads us to the truth. The Holy Spirit builds community. The Holy Spirit has been with all people in all times but has not always been welcomed or listened to by us. The voice of the Holy Spirit is recognizable because it always speaks to us of love, joy, peace, hope, patience, faithfulness, self-control, truth, generosity, and God.

12. It is the supreme gift of God because the Holy Spirit is God with us. The Holy Spirit is the Spirit of Christ because he was filled with the Holy Spirit. The Spirit of Christ is available to each of us to invite into our lives. The Spirit works to transform us into new beings, born from above. The Holy Spirit shows us the way home.

Our pilgrimage is not a journey of time or space, it is a journey into reality. This present moment is where you can and will find God.

❧

You are God's favorite! This truth was explained to me in the company of Jesus Christ and the angels of heaven. Within our perception of the finite nature of the world, being favored and giving favor is choosing one over the many, but in God's infinite capacity for love, God favors each of us just as we are. This is one of the most important lessons that my teachers were trying to teach me. God has the capacity to know us intimately and love us passionately just as we are. God created us to be wonderful.

To become the beautiful people God has created us to be, we have to wake up from our dream that separates us from the reality of God. We are spiritual beings having a physical experience. This brief event we call life is neither our beginning nor our end. In heaven we will look back upon our lives with the same amusement that we feel when we look at our childhood hopes and fears.

Why didn't I say "Yes" to God sooner? Why did I wait so long? How much of my life have I wasted with my eyes closed to the truth?

Yes, I need to be known.

Yes, I want to be loved for who I am.

Yes, I belong to God above all else.

Yes, you love me even though I denied you.

Yes, by your power I can change my life.

Yes, I welcome you in my heart, making me a new person.

In your great love for us, you forgive us and call us by name.

If you make one step toward God, God will take a giant step to you. Let God be your God.

Jesus is the way, the truth, and the life. He is the best friend you will ever have.

AFTERWORD

Serving the church as pastor has never been dull. The church is involved with the lives of people from their birth to their death, and everything in between. In the life of the church, we see the best of people and worst of people since everything that people are comes in the door of the church. What people see on Sunday is only a small fraction of what happens in ministry. The Sunday morning worship is a time for people to give their best and to be on their best behavior for the glorification of God. During the rest of the week, everything that human beings do to themselves and to one another demands the attention of the pastor. If one enjoys human drama and being engaged in the lives of people, it is extremely rewarding. It is difficult to imagine that one could be the church pastor without the constant encouragement and support of the Holy Spirit. It is necessary to rely upon the Spirit of Christ to know what to say, and when to listen. The role of the pastor is to love people as they are, and not demand that they change before they are lovable. It is also the role of the pastor to encourage people to change according to the will of the Holy Spirit.

The biggest challenge that I have found in pastoring a church has been raising the consciousness of the congregation toward compassion for people beyond the boundaries of the church. The work of the church is not simply to comfort the members of the church; rather, the work of the church is to be like Christ to the world. The world consists mostly of people who do not know God or Christ and could care less. As Jesus spent his life going out to the world and sending his disciples out into the world, so the church must do likewise. For reasons that I do not fully understand, I have found this difficult for many Christians to appreciate.

For the past several years I have been leading mission groups to work with the Maya of Belize, Central America. Many of these beautiful people have been marginalized from the global economy to live subsistence lives. We have had the opportunity to significantly impact their lives through improvements to their schools, substantial improvement in their health care, improving their living conditions, and, most important, encouraging their faith development. The overwhelming majority of people that we work with there belong to the Roman Catholic Church, and we have been blessed with a wonderful working relationship between the Catholic Church and a number of different Christian denominations that support this ministry. We experience a sign of the Kingdom of God as we work together without denominational differences. The people who have gone on these mission trips have received spiritual riches from the people that we serve far beyond the material gifts that we bring to them.

When we make our small sacrifices to serve God, we are encouraged and rewarded by God with spiritual gifts far in excess of what we deserve. This is God's way of raising us to become the children of God we were created to be. As Jesus so amply demonstrated to us, the only way to grow spiritually is by serving others.

ACKNOWLEDGMENTS

Anne Rice was instrumental in the publication of this book in the United States. I am deeply grateful for her support of my testimony and the desire to make it available to the public. Anne is a woman of huge accomplishments as an author, and more important, someone who has persevered in her spiritual journey toward God through many trials. It has been a privilege to share my story with her and for her to share some of her story with me. We have so many coincidences in our lives that it is no wonder there is a bond between us. She has been a Godsend in my life and I pray she will be blessed for the work we both have done.